KT-133-177

CONTENTS

ACKNOWLEDGEMENTS

Human wisdom depends on many things, among which human interaction and personal reflection are paramount. This short book owes much to many people. It is dedicated to the late Dr Maura Daly, who was the first person to research suicide and deliberate self-poisoning in Munster.

The members of the burgeoning Suicide Research Foundation have each endeavoured to make this short book a success. Sinéad Byrne edited and proof-read the manuscript. Dr Helen Keeley, research psychiatrist and Paul Corcoran, statistician, sharpened the scientific content. Eileen Williamson, project manager, and Ursula Burke maintained an everyday sense of balance. Kathryn Sheehan converted my halting dictation to prose.

I am also grateful to Gerald Goldberg, former Lord Mayor of Cork, for providing me with references to Judaism.

The CSO were, as ever, most facilitating and obliging towards us and our work. I would also like to thank the Department of Health, the Southern Health Board and the Mid-Western Health Board, for the funding which has made the Suicide Research Foundation possible.

All the royalties accruing to this publication will be paid directly to the Foundation, in order to advance our understanding of suicide and parasuicide.

MICHAEL J. KELLEHER
1 JANUARY 1996

FOREWORD

It is important that we understand the tragic problem of suicide in a specific Irish context. It can no longer be ignored. Decriminalisation, which I canvassed for over many years, is not enough. It is a small important start. We must identify the reasons why our young and old seek to end their lives in such a terribly sad way.

Suicidal behaviour is a great drain on the individual himself, his family, the health services and the wealth of the nation. A means must be found to limit these losses. The successful suicide is one of the most devastating events to occur in a family and locality. We must understand the trauma and stress that the bereaved suffer. We must respond to assist them.

It is for these reasons, and many others, that I welcome Michael J. Kelleher's book, which draws together many strands of research and clinical practice. It is written in a very personal way, through which his humanity shines.

SENATOR DAN NEVILLE
SEANAD ÉIREANN

NOTE

The use of 'he', 'him', 'his' and 'himself' has been adopted throughout the book, to refer to either sex, where a singular pronoun of common gender has been required. The reason for this is simply to avoid clumsiness, especially when the pronouns have to be repeated frequently. There is no sexist bias or offence intended.

INTRODUCTION

There was a time when suicide was neither considered nor discussed openly. It was hidden and shameful. The victim was buried quickly and with as little fuss as possible. Strangely, this was an advance on the attitudes of earlier generations, when a suicide was feared as someone or something that embodied evil. This notion of evilness precluded church burial in sanctified ground. In some parts of western Europe, the remains were publicly dishonoured. Examples included burying the dead face-downwards, doing so at a crossroad and driving a stake through the heart.

Much of this had to do with the concept of the soul and what happened to it when it wholly rejected the love of God. The ancient belief was that, at death, the soul emerged from the mouth to face divine judgement, but that among evil people this might not happen. In the case of Pontius Pilate, folklore had it that the soul emerged through his anus. Such an evil and restless spirit might bring harm to the living. Burial at the cross-road may have been seen as a step towards confusing an evil spirit and preventing its return. Furthermore, the crossroad was in public rather than private ownership, so that the evil would not be visited upon any one individual.

This fearful and condemnatory attitude to suicide did not always exist. There are a number of suicides described in the Old Testament of the Bible. The methods are clearly described, but no criticism is made.

One example is when Saul, the first King of Israel, fought and lost a battle against the Philistines. His three sons were killed and he himself was wounded. All was lost. He asked his armour-bearer to kill him, rather than allow the Philistines to do so. The armour-bearer refused, whereupon Saul fell on his sword killing himself. His servant then did likewise.[1]

A further example is when Ahithophel sided with Absalom in a revolt against King David. Absalom was defeated. When Ahithophel realised the likely outcome, he went home and hanged himself there. The prospect of military defeat also caused the suicide of Zimri. After the capture of the city of Tirzah, the hopelessness of the situation led him to decide to burn himself to death in the flames of the King's house, which he set on fire. And Samson's death was also suicide, although it had the political advantage of causing destruction to those Philistines gathered in the Temple of Dagon.

A poignant mass suicide of Jews occurred in the first century. After their army was overrun by the Romans, the remaining soldiers petitioned their general, Josephus, to allow them to kill themselves en masse. He counselled against this. What was left of the army retreated to Masada, without Josephus, and held out for several years against the Roman legions. Eventually, when all appeared lost, the 960 survivors ended their lives on the towering rock fortress that they had defended. It is likely that those who did not choose death voluntarily were murdered by their peers. Unfortunately, Masada proved a hallowed, if lethal model for harassed Jews in later centuries.[2] The most notorious mass suicide occurred in York in 1190 during a pogrom. There are many other examples throughout European history, although, strangely, mass suicide did not feature prominently during the holocaust. There were, however, cases of Jewish girls being poisoned by their teachers in preference to being raped by soldiers.[3]

Suicide for political reasons was not unknown to the Celt. When Attalus I defeated the Celts in Asia Minor, he erected statues to celebrate his victory. In one of these, a young, handsome Gaul is depicted as stabbing himself through the chest, having already slain his wife.[4] Celtic soldiers were also said to take a vow to die with their leader even if this meant killing themselves.[5]

Hunger strike is the preferred Irish method of political suicide. Voluntary starvation, particularly by older men, was regarded as a dignified manner of death in ancient Greece and Rome.[6] The best-known Irish hunger striker was Terence MacSwiney, Lord Mayor of Cork, who in response to what he regarded as wrongful imprisonment, announced that he would be free within thirty days. This was the period that was then believed by the medical profession to be the longest time a starving man could survive. In fact, he lived seventy-three days. De Valera, who was a staunchly conservative Catholic, encouraged him to persist in the fast. Fr Dominic O'Connor was present on a daily basis in his prison cell, joining him in prayer and often celebrating mass. Dr Daniel Mannix, Archbishop of Melbourne (my grandmother's first cousin), visited him twice in prison. More than any other event, apart from the execution of the leaders of the 1916 rebellion, his persistence in starving himself turned world opinion against the continued occupation of Ireland.[7] My late father, Denis P. Kelleher, who was a commander in the old IRA, orchestrated part of his public funeral and so I am emotionally familiar with the mood of the time.

Terence MacSwiney was honoured with the complete public rites of the Catholic Church. This demonstrates the inconsistent attitude of the Church towards suicide. Two bishops and some four hundred clergy jammed St George's Cathedral, London, for the funeral mass. Three bishops officiated at the mass in Dublin the following day. Bishop Coholan not only officiated at the funeral mass in Cork, but also described Terence MacSwiney as a martyr, in an open letter to *The Cork Examiner*. Bishop Coholan, however, was inconsistent. He subsequently refused the rites of Christian burial to a hunger striker, Dennis Barry, following the Civil War.[7] The attitude and behaviour of the Irish Catholic hierarchy are redolent of the earlier behaviour of the Anglican episcopacy, following the suicide of Lord Castlereagh.[8]

No one suggested then, or since then, that 'the balance of his mind was upset', which was the common 'let-out' phrase used to allow burial in sanctified ground. Many people then (and perhaps still now), including my late father, would have been offended if the word suicide was used to describe his death. Yet, there is no other way to describe what happened. He voluntarily embarked upon a course of action in the full knowledge that it would bring about his own death. Such is the definition

of suicide. The fact that he was motivated by noble, political ends is not at issue.

Mahatma Gandhi admired MacSwiney. As is well-
known, Gandhi entered into a public fast which resulted
in great political change in the sub-continent of India.[9]

Many others went on hunger strike during the time
of the Rising – some of whom died while being forcibly
fed. However, the most recent 'political suicide' in Ireland
to have been given martyr status, is that of Bobby
Sands.[10] Such deaths require obsessional resoluteness
and determination.

There is a parallel with anorexia nervosa. Recently, I
saw a fourteen-year-old girl who had reduced her weight
from nine stone to seven in a matter of weeks. She told
me that she intended to persist in her non-eating behaviour, even though, as she said herself, death would be
the outcome.

Most suicides, however, are lonely, hidden affairs
occurring far away from the blaze of publicity. Those who
die are usually ill, even if they end their lives on impulse.
Irrational suicides are rare. Most are not psychotic, to
use the modern anodyne phrase for 'mad'. Yet, in dying,
they throw away the miracle of individual existence that
can never be recreated, no matter how many more bil-
lions of people are born. Often the death is, to use a
catchphrase, a permanent solution to a temporary problem.

This book is an attempt to address this problem in
the context of Ireland. We are an island people. In the
past, we appeared to have been relatively insulated from
suicide. However, as the succeeding chapters will show,

13

this has changed and we have a responsibility to find out why. Academic knowledge, however, is not enough. Two other things must also be done; if possible, suicide and attempted suicide must be prevented and the turmoil of the bereaved must be assuaged.

1

THE RISE IN SUICIDE

At the time of the re-invasion of Europe towards the end of the Second World War, one of the generals involved is said to have retorted when given new conflicting information, that he did not wish to be 'bothered by facts', as he had already decided on a course of action. Such a bluff tough-guy approach is inappropriate in the study of suicide. Facts are everything. How we define them is central to our understanding. Much of the variation in suicide rates across countries may be, in part, a consequence of how unnatural deaths are categorised. In some countries, claims are made that the suicide rate is falling, due to planned social intervention. In truth, the rates of undetermined deaths are rising, which is the likely explanation as to why the official suicide rates are in decline.

Ireland had the lowest rate of suicide in Europe at one time. It was assumed by researchers in some, more powerful countries, that the Irish figures were purposely fudged. In other words, it was assumed that there was a great tendency among the Irish, either at local or central level, to label suicides as accidental deaths.

There is evidence that suicide has been under-reported in the past and may still be in some areas of the country.[1] One study done in Dublin almost thirty years ago indicated this.[2] A further study, done in the Galway area ten years ago, also disclosed under-reporting.[3]

Under-reporting, however, is not a uniquely Irish phenomenon. It can, and does occur in all countries. A recent study of railway suicides in London, found that many deaths where the individual was seen clearly and purposefully stepping off the platform into the path of the oncoming train, were subsequently adjudged as non-suicide in the coroners' court.[4]

A conjoint study by the Central Statistics Office and the Southern Health Board, suggests that the official suicide rate may be under-reporting the true rate by some 15% to 20%.[5, 6] A major problem in the definition of suicide is the determination of intention. With some methods of death, such as drowning and self-poisoning, this is particularly difficult. The best approach to adopt is one based on the balance of probabilities.[4, 7]

If the low suicide rate among the Irish in the past could be explained by under-reporting, then one would expect that when the Irish emigrated to other countries, this 'spurious' low suicide rate would have no longer been evident. However, this was not so – the incidence of suicide remained low among Irish emigrants to the United States and Australia.[8, 9] When thirteen emigrant groups to the United States were compared in rank order of suicide, the Irish were positioned twelfth, just ahead of the Mexicans. The implication is that whatever the cultural–protective factors of the time were, they were internalised so as to allow them to continue to protect the individual, even when living in other countries. It is true to say, however, that the Irish abroad had a higher rate than the Irish at home.

Unfortunately, all of this has changed (Figures 1.1 and 1.2). As can be seen, the rise in the rate of suicide cannot be explained by a fall in the rates of accidental drowning, accidental poisoning and undetermined deaths.

During the 1970s, the Irish population increased for the first time since the Famine – largely due to the return of emigrants, as well as immigrants from other countries. Theoretically, for any age group or overall, it is possible that an increase in the number of suicides could simply be a reflection of the increase in the population. Expressing the rate per 100,000 population takes any such population changes into account and thus accurately reflects the incidence of suicide.

By statistical tradition, all deaths are divided into those caused by illness (natural deaths) and those not caused directly by illness (unnatural deaths). Unnatural deaths are further sub-divided into a number of categories; including accidental poisoning, accidental drowning, road traffic accidents, accidental falls, suicide (where the individual is believed to have purposefully brought about his own death), and undetermined deaths (where it is unclear whether the individual accidentally or deliberately brought about his own death). Three studies have concluded that the rise in suicide in Ireland is genuine and not a result of reclassification of unnatural deaths. Nonetheless, it is true to say that the confidential garda reports to the CSO and the greater openness of Irish society have helped to bring about a more accurate

17

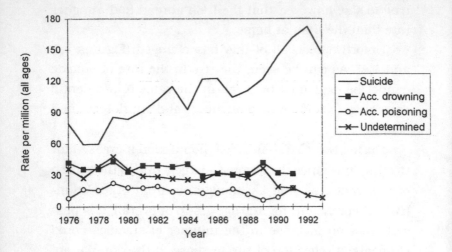

Figure 1.1. Irish male rate of suicide, accidental drowning,
accidental poisoning and undetermined death, 1976–93.
[Source: CSO Dept of Vital Statistics]

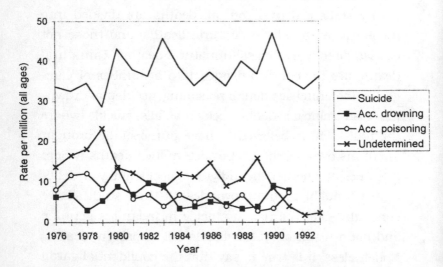

Figure 1.2. Irish female rate of suicide, accidental drowning,
accidental poisoning and undetermined death, 1976–93.
[Source: CSO Dept of Vital Statistics]

division of unnatural deaths.[10, 11, 12]

The most striking rise has been in young male suicides (Figure 1.3).[13] Thankfully, there has been no such rise among young Irish females (Figure 1.4). In order to show where we stand internationally, comparisons have been made with four other countries for the 15–24 year age-groups. Finland was chosen as a country that had one of the highest rates of suicide in Europe. Japan and the United States were chosen because they represented those countries with medium rates. Ireland with England and Wales represent the group with the lowest rates.

The contrast between Japan and Ireland is striking – the Irish male rate has gradually risen so that we have now joined the Americans in the medium group, whereas Japan's rate has fallen so that they have joined the lowest group. The implication of the Japanese figures, if genuine, is that technological advancement does not have to mean an inexorable rise in suicide. This may be related to changes in the Japanese educational system, which have been made so that the young are better prepared to face a more uncertain future.

The divergent patterns of suicide among young Irish males and females raise important issues. They suggest that whatever stresses our young people encounter, boys are more vulnerable than girls. However, it should be added that world-wide, men are more predisposed to suicide than women are. There are a few exceptions to this, for example elderly women in Hungary and some Asiatic women.[14]

However, this world-wide male/female divergence is

19

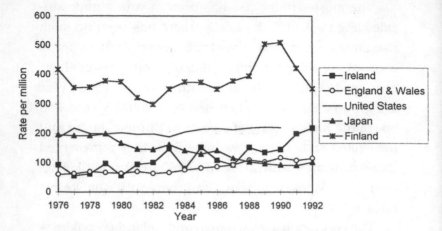

Figure 1.3. International suicide rates for 15–24 year-old males, 1976–92. [Source: WHO Yearly Statistics, 1976–92]

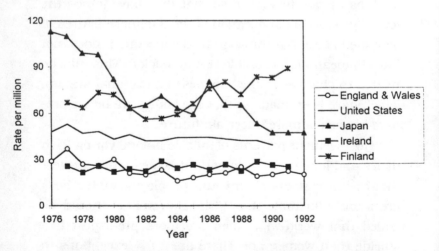

Figure 1.4. International suicide rates for 15–24 year-old females, 1976–92. [Source: WHO Yearly Statistics, 1976–92] Note: due to the volatility of the Finnish and Irish rates, 3-year moving averages were used.

20

not sufficient to explain the rise in suicide among young Irish men. Most western democracies have seen a rise in young male suicides. Two factors may have contributed to the situation at home – the first of these, being related to the individual, is likely to be shared with the young world-wide, while the second relates to changes in Irish social and cultural life. Nonetheless, one is probably influenced by the other, particularly now that, with modern technology, we are increasingly participants in a shared world-village life.

Some have argued that the rise in suicide is related to a change in illness-pattern. The evidence for this is not striking. Puberty now occurs, on average, at 12.5 years, as opposed the 14.2 years of the beginning of the century.[15] Depression amongst the under-25s is much more common today than it was 90 years ago.[16] This has been related to the lower onset-age of puberty, but is not thought to be a biological effect; when adolescent boys and girls are individually examined, the age at which puberty begins does not affect the likelihood of depression.[17]

If adolescence is construed as the period between puberty and one's first adult job, then the length of adolescence has greatly increased throughout the twentieth century. My late father was eighteen or nineteen when he joined 'The Movement'. One of his associates was in his late twenties – my father told me that he and his colleagues regarded him as an old man. Many young people today do not attain even relative economic independence until their early twenties. All must stay at school until sixteen. When given employment, it is often poorly paid,

21

uncertain and of low status.

It is one contention of this book that such forces have a worse effect on young men than on young women. In this context, it is assumed that a depressed person today is more likely to consider suicide an option than would a similarly depressed person some thirty years ago.

Older men, unlike women of all age-groups, also show a pronounced rise in suicide.[18] Over the past two decades, 65–75 year-old men have been particularly vulnerable. One hundred cases of suicide, which have appeared before the two Cork city coroners, have been examined by the Suicide Research Foundation as part of a psychological autopsy study (see Chapter 5 for more detailed discussion on this). Of these, twelve (six men and six women) were aged over 65.[19] Five men had never married and the sixth had learned of his wife's terminal illness prior to his suicide. For them, isolation would seem to have been especially important. All six women were known to be psychiatrically ill and three of them had been bereaved of their spouses some time before their suicides.

It is also important to realise that suicide may have different causes in young and old, in men and women. If we are to address the problem effectively, we will need different strategies for the different age-groups. Throughout the succeeding pages, possible protective and risk factors will be explored.

2

RELIGION AND SUICIDE

Over the past thirty years, Ireland has gone through a cultural and social revolution. There have been profound changes in the fabric of society. Nowhere is this more obvious than in the area of religion, which has witnessed changes in practice, worship and belief. Such changes may have influenced attitudes towards suicide.

It is almost a hundred years since the great French sociologist, Emile Durkheim, published his book on suicide.[1] Among other things, he quoted rates of suicide from different parts of the German-speaking world; when the suicide rates were expressed per million, Catholics invariably showed lower rates of suicide than Protestants. He then examined suicide in Switzerland and found that for both French and German-speaking cantons, the suicide rate amongst the Protestants was approximately four times higher than the rate amongst the Catholics.[2]

Durkheim regarded the Catholic religion as a protective factor against suicide. He believed that predominantly Catholic countries had lower suicide rates than predominantly Protestant ones. He found England to have an intermediate rate; and this he attributed to the manner of worship within the Anglican Church, which he believed had retained many of the practices of Catholicism. Durkheim, who himself was a Jew, saw the Protestant as a person who stood in a direct relationship with God. Whereas the Catholic, in his view, had many mediating factors; including a sacramental priesthood, communal worship and confession. He did not mention the Catholic Church's condemnatory attitude towards suicide, which may also have been important.

Recent work has shown that religious denomination, even if one is non-practising, does influence suicide rates. A study of suicide in Holland confirms that traditionally Catholic areas have lower rates of suicide than traditionally Protestant areas, even though church-attendance by both Catholics and Protestants is minimal.[3] One Dutch Protestant sect, called the Orthodox Christians, had lower rates than Dutch Catholics. These people live and practise their faith actively in the light of the New Testament.

A further confirmation of the importance of religion comes from the study of emigrants to the United States. Those with the lowest suicide rates came from Catholic countries.[4] And, if one looks at the 'suicide map' of Europe, Catholic countries generally return lower suicide rates than Protestant ones do.[5]

What relevance does this have to the changing Irish suicide rate? Some 94% of the citizens of the Irish Republic are Catholic, and if Catholicism is protective, then Ireland should have a low rate of suicide by comparison with neighbouring Britain.[6] This was the case in the past.[7] However, the grip of the Catholic Church on the minds of the people has weakened over the past two or three decades.

24

One could argue that a survey is not needed to confirm religious change in Ireland. All one needs to do is to visit and participate in church worship, as my family and I do. It is rare now to sit in an overcrowded church. The sparse congregation is likely to be old rather than young, and with more women than men. Church-attendance is lower in urban areas than in rural ones; the middle class out-number other social groups; and third level students attend church less often than their non-student peers.

Belief in central religious authority is waning in Ireland. Despite the direct intervention of the Pope, the 1995 divorce referendum was marginally passed. This contrasts with the 1986 referendum, when divorce was rejected by a majority of 2:1.

There have been a number of major studies of Irish beliefs and practices since 1974.[6, 8, 9] Table 2.1 shows the changes in religious beliefs among Irish Roman Catholics between 1974 and 1984 – the most significant change being a doubling in the numbers of those unsure as to their beliefs.

Those who were unsure that the Roman Catholic Church was the one true Church increased from 8.9% to 19.8%. At the same time, those who doubted that the Bible was the word of God increased from 11.3% to 22.2%. The proportion who doubted papal infallibility increased from 17.9% to 29.3%.

While most people in Ireland, in 1984, believed in the reality of sin, 20.6% doubted or rejected the idea that confession forgives sin. This compares with 12.8% in 1974. Belief in the reality of hell also diminished during this period. In 1974, only half the population (51.3%) believed that there was such a place as hell, which is surprising in view of the many sermons on sin and damnation then. By 1984, this figure had fallen to 41.1%.[8]

All the great religions have taken a keen interest in suicide and its moral implications.[10] This is particularly so with Judaism, Christianity and Islam.[11] From a Christian point of view, it was in the fourth century that St Augustine redefined the commandment 'Thou shalt not kill', to include the killing of the self.[10] As discussed in a later chapter on the morality of suicide, intentional self-killing became a sin; not just an ordinary sin, but a most grievous one, because it threw the gift of life back into God's face. Traditional Christian worship focused on four things: death, judgement, heaven and hell. Of these, only death is now certain. The rest is open to debate and speculation.

Father Micheál Mac Gréil compared the findings of his 1988–1989 study with those of Breslin and Weafer (1984) and the Catholic bishop's survey (1974).[6, 8] Mac Gréil reported a fall-off in attendance at weekly Mass and monthly communion, as well as a more profound fall-off in monthly confessions (Figure 2.1). By 1995, the number of those making monthly confessions had further declined.[9] Apart from spiritual considerations, confession allowed the individual to bare his inner troubles. It may have had a protective effect. Analogies are frequently drawn between psychiatrists and priests. It is not unusual for a psychiatrist to be absent-mindedly addressed as 'Father', during a one-to-one therapeutic en-

	Fully Accept		Unsure		Reject	
	1974	1984	1974	1984	1974	1984
Belief in Authority						
Papal infallibility	68.8%	60.8%	17.9%	29.3%	13.3%	9.9%
RC is the true church	82.9%	73.0%	8.9%	19.8%	8.2%	7.1%
Bible is word of God	85.2%	75.7%	11.3%	22.2%	3.4%	2.1%
Sin, Confession & Damnation						
Belief in sin		91.8%		7.0%		1.2%
Confession forgives sin	87.2%	79.3%	7.4%	16.4%	5.4%	4.2%
Belief in Hell	51.3%	41.1%	22.0%	39.7%	26.8%	19.1%

Table 2.1. Changes in religious belief among Irish Roman Catholics, 1974 and 1984.
Note: 1974 sample of 2,499 respondents; 1984 sample of 1,006 respondents.
[Source: Breslin & Weafer, *Religious beliefs, practices and moral attitudes*, 1986]

27

counter with a patient.

Mac Gréil also looked at the prayer habit of those in his study, according to age and gender (Table 2.2). The figures show that the young pray less than the old, and that men pray less than women. It would appear from the tables shown that Catholics in Ireland are becoming increasingly less religious. One opinion poll indicates that most people do not go to confession now, even on a yearly basis.[9] The change in *weltanschauung* or general outlook on life, from the religious to the secular, must affect how we Irish respond to stress. As religion loses its hold, its capacity to allow sublimation of troubles and disappointment diminishes.

	Several times a day	At least once a day	At least several times a week	At least once a week	Less than once a week	Number
Age						
18-20yrs	19%	48%	76%	89%	11%	54
21-35yrs	22%	59%	74%	86%	14%	321
36-50yrs	33%	73%	84%	91%	9%	248
51yrs+	62%	90%	94%	97%	3%	320
Gender						
Males	31%	64%	76%	87%	13%	425
Females	44%	80%	89%	94%	6%	518

Table 2.2. Frequency of prayer among Irish Roman Catholics by age and gender, 1988–89. [Source: Mac Gréil, M., *Religious Practice and Attitudes in Ireland*, p. 36, 1991]

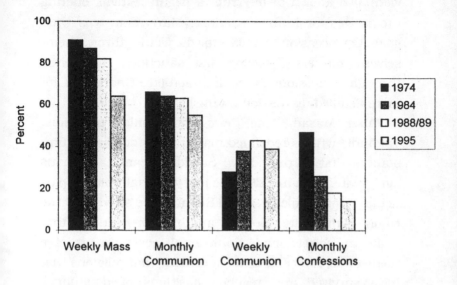

Figure 2.1. Fall-off in Catholic worship, 1974–95. [Sources: Mac Gréil, M., *Religious Practice and Attitudes in Ireland* (p. 21), 1991; *Sunday Independent*, 5 November, 1995]

Not just Irish society, but society world-wide is restively seeking a philosophy to explain and alleviate psychic pain.

Whilst religion does have some protective influence, it is not necessarily protective against suicide. Both Judaism and Christianity have had an ambivalent attitude towards martyrdom. Suicide is strictly prohibited according to Islam. It was, however, traditionally acceptable for a Muslim to 'run amok' and kill infidels, until he himself was killed.[12] This is not dissimilar to the activities of the Donatists, against whom Augustine railed. It was not uncommon for the Donatists to challenge a magistrate to either kill them, or be killed himself.[13] They were also known to interrupt a pagan festival, offering themselves for human sacrifice. Martyrdom was their goal. On occasion, whole crowds would throw themselves from cliffs, having first sanctified themselves through confession and communion (see Chapter 11 for more detailed discussion on this).

After Masada, the Jews had similar problems. Talmudic writers redefined martyrdom and the circumstances that permitted it.[14] Suicide became a heinous sin; greater than murder. The fear was that suicide, particularly mass suicide, could threaten the survival of the whole community. Society and the institutions that make up society, endeavour, at all costs, to preserve themselves. Hence, it is not surprising that religions that have survived and reached positions of dominance throughout the centuries, should have adopted a position where suicide is anathema. Such is the case with Judaism, Christianity and Islam.

3

SUICIDE AND FAMILY LIFE

Freud saw religion as a projection of obsessional neurosis.[1] Durkheim saw God as a deification of society.[2] Both were engaged in a type of territorial defence and each saw himself as having created a new scientific domain. For Freud, it was a dynamic psychology and for Durkheim, a dynamic sociology. The latter may have been influenced by the great French physiologist, Claude Bernard, whose many contributions to medicine included the concept of the *milieu interior*. Durkheim elaborated a social *milieu exterior*, incorporating several forces or currents which he believed impinged on the individual and yet, were independent of him.

Durkheim's two great sociological forces were regulation and integration. He theorised that too little regulation led to anomy; too much regulation led to fatalism; too little integration led to egoism; and too much integration led to altruism – effects which were in turn associated with suicide. These forces were believed by him to be in a vibrant flux, determining a relatively constant rate of suicide for each society studied.

The most intimate and forceful social-milieu that each one of us is exposed to, is family life. Most of us are born into a family from which we emerge in adult life and most of us then seek to create our own families, once we have the power and opportunity to do so. Family structure may influence the likelihood of suicide.[3]

Until recently, the extended family was a reality. My father had ninety-three first cousins and he knew them all. Few moved from West Cork. Daniel Corkery, who was a personal friend of Terence MacSwiney's, was probably right when he noted that the Irish had a predominant attachment to place.[4] Traditional Gaelic bardic poetry is rich in tír-grá, or poetry devoted to love of country or place. This attachment to both place and family has provided Irish people with a solid sense of belonging.

My own generation is the generation of the nuclear-family. Nowadays, there are few reasons for extended family gatherings, apart from deaths and marriages. The last two decades have witnessed significant change in family life in Ireland (Figure 3.1). The marriage rate has been falling, while the number of unmarried couples in cohabitation has been rising.

In 1971, only 3% of children were born outside of wedlock. By 1992, this figure had risen to 18%.[5] In some sections of society, particularly the urban poor, this proportion is much higher. From 1976 to 1993, the adoption rate fell from 23 to 7 per 50,000 population.[6] These two trends confirm that the number of unmarried mothers is increasing, and that they are assuming full-responsibility for the care of their children.

Between 1986 and 1991, the percentage of the population who were formally separated from their spouses greatly increased.[5] At the time of writing, the very restrictive divorce referendum has just been passed by a small majority. Now that divorce is allowed, it is likely that this increase will become significantly greater.

A study of suicide in eighteen countries showed a close correlation between the suicide and divorce rates.[7] Whereas marriage has a protective influence on the mental health of men, it is less protective of that of women. One Irish study showed that, among other things, unmarried Irish women had fewer obsessional symptoms than married ones had.[8]

Durkheim noted, a hundred years ago, that female suicide was inversely proportional to the number of children they had.[9] If it is true that children protect women

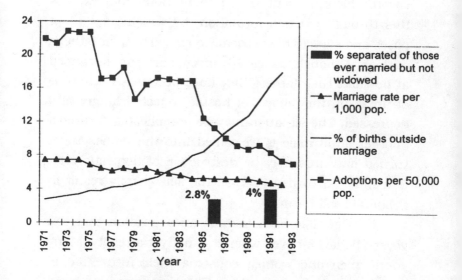

Figure 3.1. Marriage, separation, adoption, and births outside marriage in Ireland, 1971–93. [Sources: CSO census report, 1986 and 1991; CSO vital statistics: yearly summary, 1971–92; An Bord Uchtála yearly report, 1993]

from suicide, then this effect is presumably decreasing, because the average number of children born to women is falling.[5] The highest rates of suicide among Irish women occur for the late middle-aged and older. One reason for this is the increasing level of psychological illness in these age-bands. Another might be the 'empty nest syndrome', where a mother feels a sense of loss of social function and purpose when her children leave home.

The increasing instability of nuclear-family life may have a more deleterious effect on the adolescent male than on the adolescent female. If the home breaks up, it is usually the father who leaves. Most boys are overtly or covertly identified with their fathers. Some may express this through reaction formation, by which they adopt poses and stances diametrically opposed to their father's outlook. Although, as age advances, many are surprised at how like their fathers they have become. At the time of break-up they may feel hostile, rejected, angry and depressed. The situation may be complicated further if another adult male is welcomed into the home. Anger turned outwards may be destructive of domestic relationships.[10] If turned in upon the self, it may result in deliberate self-harm.

Marriage, like patriotism, is an aspiration that can govern behaviour even when it is not yet a reality. Many young men and women construe their future life in terms of marital relationships. This presupposes a belief in one's capacity to love and to engender love in another. Men, however, may feel ever more excluded from domestic life, as women increasingly conceive outside of marriage and less frequently hand their babies over for adoption. It is right that the mother and child should receive state aid. An unseen consequence of this provision, however, may be to make the man feel rejected.

Not only is bonding the cement of society, it is also the oxygen essential to the person. As the book of Genesis said, 'it is not good for man to be alone'. We all need a soul-mate. Those who have such a soul-mate are protected. Claims have been made that suicide and attempted suicide are more prevalent among the gay and lesbian communities.[11] If this were so, then one reason might be the transience of relationships where society at large does not have a vested interest in their maintenance.

Recently, the professional parents of a clever adolescent who had hanged himself a few weeks previously, came to see me because of their distress and bewilderment. One of the questions they asked of me, was whether their son might have had difficulties relating to his sexual orientation, unbeknownst to them. Among the many other problems they must face, adolescents have to reach an understanding with themselves as to how they are going to use and control their natural sexual instincts. This is the case whether heterosexual or homosexual. It is claimed that homosexual youths have special difficulties, particularly if they 'come out'. The process of coming out has four interlocking-dimensions: the recognition that one is predominantly or exclusively gay or lesbian; expressing this knowledge in the context of the gay community; disclosing one's orientation to significant others; and finally acceptance of one's orientation with a sense of equilibrium.[11]

The issue of the relationship between homosexuality and suicidal behaviour is far from clear, however.[12] Basically, the research data on which these hypotheses about homosexuality are based, are poor. The deficiencies include matters of definition and design. To date, in Ireland, there has been no study of suicide among the gay community.

There is a danger in reading too much into the association between trends in suicide, religious practice and family life. This centres on what is called the 'ecological fallacy', which contends that what is true for groups, may not be true for the individuals within the group. Originally postulated over forty years ago, it was pointedly criticised twenty-five years later.[13, 14] There are three possibilities: that the changes in religious practice and family life are wholly unrelated to changes in suicide rates; that somehow they are instrumental in bringing the changes about; or that other factors underlie the changes in these three areas. Only more focused research will clarify these issues.[10]

4

ADOLESCENT STRESS AND YOUTH SUICIDE

Scripture tells us that we must work out our salvation through fear and trembling. Whatever about the next world, this is certainly true of the one we live in and it is especially true of adolescence. We emerge from our parental and family environment and we must establish our own sense of purpose and meaning in adult life. Traditional societies have clear-cut and well-defined *rites de passage*, while the secular, modern world offers many invitations, but little purposeful direction.

Suicide is now the second most common cause of death, after road traffic accidents, among 15 to 24 year-old Irish males (Figure 4.1).[1] Between 1976 and 1978, the rates of suicide and cancer deaths among young men were almost equal. However, in each successive three-year period, suicide increased and from 1982, cancer deaths began to decrease. Between 1991 and 1993, the rate of suicide was almost two and a half times that of cancer deaths (Figure 4.2). Surely, what can be done for cancer can be done for suicide?

It has been argued that in relation to suicide there is an element of choice involved, whereas with cancer among the young there is none. With cancer deaths among older people there may be a degree of choice,

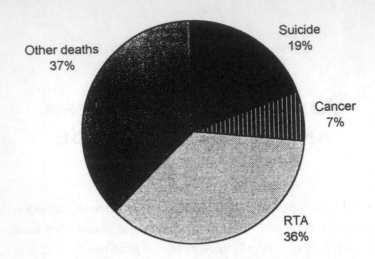

Figure 4.1. Cause of death for 15–24 year-old Irish males, 1991–93. [Source: CSO vital statistics: yearly summary, 1991–93]

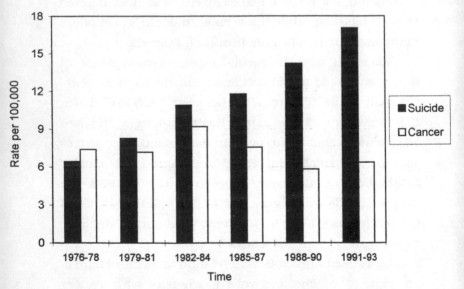

Figure 4.2. Suicide rate versus rate of cancer deaths for 15–24 year-old Irish males. [Source: CSO Dept of Vital Statistics]

insofar as some deaths are related to nicotine and even alcohol. The argument that less can be done about suicide than about cancer, due to the element of choice, does not stand up if one examines road traffic deaths, where human error, if not human choice, is a significant factor.

Between 1976 and 1978, there were eight times as many road traffic deaths as suicides among young men. Since 1980, however, the rate of road traffic deaths has fallen, whereas the suicide rate has continued to rise. This means that road traffic deaths are now only about twice as common as suicides (Figure 4.3).

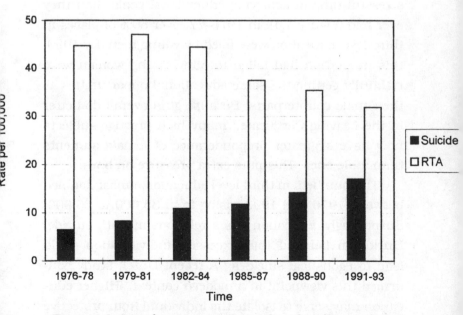

Figure 4.3. Suicide rate versus rate of road traffic accident deaths for 15–24 year-old Irish males. [Source: CSO Dept of Vital Statistics]

In other countries, where road traffic deaths are less prevalent, the suicide rate equals the road traffic death rate. There are many reasons as to why the rate of road traffic deaths has fallen, all involving human endeavour; these include better roads, better cars, better assessment of drivers, continued education of the public, restrictions on speed, and more stringent laws on alcohol usage. The cost, which has been truly enormous, is paying off. Suicide should receive a similar investment.

As has already been pointed out, the length of adolescence is increasing, due to a lowering of the onset-age of puberty and a delay in the achievement of full adult roles. Apart from this, males may now have a more stressful time in achieving educational goals than they ever had (Figure 4.4). In 1976–77, over 60% of places in third level education were filled by young men. By 1990, this proportion had fallen to 53%. Young women were rightfully getting the same educational opportunities as their male counterparts. Because girls overall do better in the Leaving Certificate,[2] many high prestige subjects now have a greater preponderance of female students than male ones. This puts extra pressure on boys.

The numbers in third level education almost doubled between 1976 and 1990, rising from 35,000 to 66,000. Surprisingly, education has a relationship with suicide. Durkheim believed that excessive individuation could lead to egotistical suicides.[3] A recent Dutch study confirmed this viewpoint in a modern context.[4] Higher education may serve to isolate the individual from protective traditions. If defences are removed, the individual is vulnerable until new coping mechanisms and attitudes are

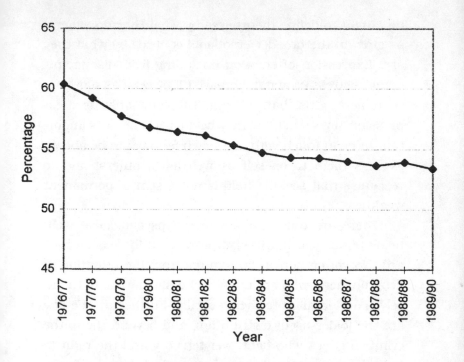

Figure 4.4. Percentage male in third level education, 1976–90.
Note: 35,047 students in third level education in 1976/77,
65,949 in third level in 1989/90. [Source: Department of
Education yearly report, 1976–90]

put in place.

Consideration must be given as to why boys are more vulnerable or susceptible to suicide than girls. It is likely that girls have traditionally received a much broader emotional education than their male counterparts did, whether within the home or at school. The male perspective, from early years, may be narrower in focus and more suited to a time when he would have held a more prestigious position within home and society. Boys may be taught to define themselves by what they do, whereas girls, in the broader emotional context, by what they are. Expression of emotion (including fear, disappointment, distress or anguish) may still be seen as more acceptable in girls than in boys. The commonly used expression 'boys don't cry' may be a lethal one. It is important to be in touch with one's own feelings; to be able to express them to oneself as well as to others, and to recognise that seeking help is not a sign of permanent weakness.[5]

There are other threats to the psychological well-being of our youth. Street drugs are an increasing hazard. No young person is immune from the attention of drug pushers, who are usually of a similar age to themselves and familiar to them socially. Further up the line are the (older-aged) distributors, and beyond them, the criminal gangs who fight over territory and the right to import, transport and manufacture illicit, mind-altering substances. Lastly, there are the skilled financiers and 'quick-buck' investors, who live a lifestyle and speak a language that the shabby pusher does not know.

There is a highly significant correlation between the youth suicide rate and the rate of drug-convictions (Figure 4.5). It is possible that this correlation is spurious, in the sense that one is not causatively related to the other, in any way. I believe that there is a relationship. There are two ways in which this could be so; firstly, some suicides may have abused drugs and secondly, the increase in street-drug usage may reflect a malaise within our society, one expression of which is an increase in deliberately self-inflicted deaths. It is also note-

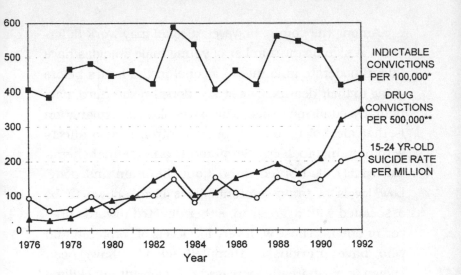

Figure 4.5. Rate of males (all ages) convicted of indictable
crime, rate of persons (male and female) convicted of drug-
related crime and 15–24 year-old male suicide rate, 1976–92.
Note: Correlation coeff. = 0.17* (not sig) and 0.89** (p-valve <
0.001). [Source: Dept of Justice: annual report, 1976–92;
CSO Dept of Vital Statistics]

worthy that there is no relationship between the frequency of indictable crimes and the youth suicide rate.
This would support the contention that there is a relationship between drug abuse and suicide.

Alcohol has a complex relationship with suicide.
Many alcoholics take their own lives, usually after several decades of alcohol abuse. This is sometimes associated with failure in all the main areas of life, whether professional, domestic or social. Getting very drunk on a
regular basis can, over time, lead to death. In a major
study of suicides in 1974, alcoholism was the most significant factor in almost one in five cases and overall,
was the second most frequent cause after depression.[6]

Among the young, however, alcohol may work differently. A significant number of young male suicides have taken moderate amounts of alcohol in the hours before going to their deaths. One study, done in Waterford, particularly confirmed this.[7] The psychological explanation is that alcohol reduces impulse control. It also affects serotonin metabolism.[8] Serotonin is an essential chemical, widely distributed throughout the brain and body. Low levels of brain-serotonin have been shown to be associated with aggression, either directed towards oneself or others. Those with very low levels of serotonin and who have previously attempted suicide, have been shown to be at greatly increased risk of eventually killing themselves.[9]

A further stress on youth is the possibility of unemployment. The job market is ever changing – few jobs now last longer than five years. The threat of unemployment and the fear of job curtailment is at least as harmful, psychologically, as actually being unemployed. It is not possible to get the rates of employment and unemployment amongst young people. However, there does appear to be an association between the young male suicide rate and the overall unemployment rate, per thousand of the labour force (Figure 4.6).[1]

Nevertheless, it is important to realise that everybody is exposed to these varied life stresses. Only a tiny minority choose suicide as a response. It is true to say that while suicide has increased, particularly among males, it is still, statistically, a rare event. Rare, but not random. This is extremely important. Illness is the probable reason for the lack of randomness in suicides. Durkheim

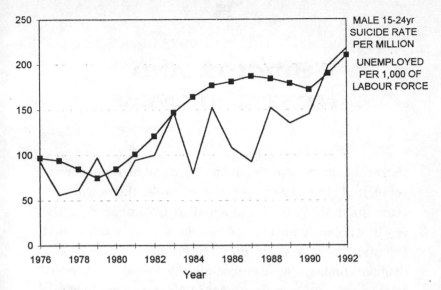

Figure 4.6. Young male suicide and unemployment. Note: Pearson correlation coefficient = 0.76 (p-value < 0.01). [Source: CSO Statistical Bulletin, 1976–92 and Dept of Vital Statistics]

was wrong to have ignored individual factors. Most suicides are likely to be mentally ill at the time of their deaths.[6] These illnesses will be discussed in the succeeding chapter.

5

SUICIDE AND
MENTAL ILLNESS

Several major studies have indicated the high prevalence
of mental illness amongst those who take their own lives.
One such study was completed in Copenhagen in the
early 1960s. Almost 1,500 suicides were studied and
mental illness was found in over 90% of the cases.[1]
Similar findings were subsequently found in Sweden,
Norway and Europe generally.[2, 3, 4] A detailed study of one
hundred suicides in Britain, done over twenty years ago,
broadly agrees with these findings.[5] Depression was present in approximately two-thirds of all cases, and alcoholism in about a fifth.

Because suicide is so alien to normal thinking, there
may be a danger of over-diagnosing mental illness, simply because the person took his own life. There ought to
be independent evidence that such illness was present.
Sometimes it is very hard to demonstrate incontrovert-
ibly that this was so. For relatives and professionals
alike, it is easier to accept a suicide in the context of illness, particularly psychological illness. We are almost
reassured to know that 'the balance of the mind' was
upset due to illness. We can accept this more easily than
the realisation that a life was lost without good reason.

Of the one hundred Irish suicides examined by the

Suicide Research Foundation (see page 22), a striking preponderance of young and early-middle-aged males can be seen (Figure 5.1).[6] The proportion of those with mental illness and those in contact with professional services is of interest.

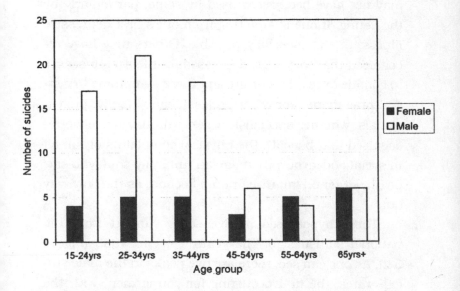

Figure 5.1. Age distribution of one hundred Cork suicides by sex. [Source: Suicide Research Foundation, Cork]

Over 80% of the women had consulted their doctors and subsequently received treatment, whereas only half of the men were in treatment at the time of their deaths. Among the men aged under-25, this proportion stood at just 20% (or one in five individuals). The proportion of those known to have mental illness was even less. These findings raise stark considerations for suicide prevention.

It is likely that the true proportion of those who were mentally ill was actually greater than our findings were able to reveal, through interview with general practitioners and surviving relatives, as well as by perusal of available hospital notes. It is also likely that mental illness may not have been recognised by some, particularly by the young. If one is suffering from one's first depressive illness, this is especially possible. Others may have recognised that they were depressed, but felt too insecure to confide in relatives or present these symptoms to general practitioners or other professionals. Finally, professionals, whether specialist or general, may not have recognised that beneath the physical complaints or fall-off in social endeavour, there lay an unhappy soul who saw death, either on impulse or on reflection, as the only way out.

These hypotheses receive some support from the national statistics for the years 1991 to 1993 (Figure 5.2). As one can see, there are two peaks in the male suicide rates: the first occurring for young men, with the second occurring for late-middle-aged men. Among women, however, the highest rates occur for the late-middle-aged. It is likely that these middle-aged people have had illnesses that have been recognised and treated, albeit unsuccessfully. It is a salutary and humbling thought that despite all the advances in psychological care in the last three decades (including better-trained doctors, well-trained voluntary workers and effective anti-depressants, both old and new) the suicide rate has still not been lowered.

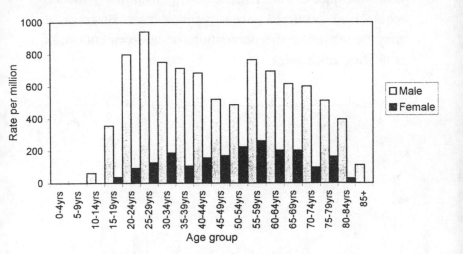

Figure 5.2. Irish male and female suicide rates in 5 year age
groups, 1991–93. [Source: CSO Dept of Vital Statistics]

The situation with young men may be different. They
could have been in their first episode of illness, unrecog-
nised by themselves, their relatives, peers and doctors.
Or, they could have been experiencing a philosophical
dilemma – a dis-ease *[sic]* of the soul, as opposed to a
medical malady or illness category. Somehow life's purpose, for them, was not worth the effort (see also p. 115).
One reflective physician has suggested that in harsher
and less settled times, such young men might have been
at the forefront in wartime situations, where risk-taking
is both institutionalised and rewarded by hero status.[7]

Something appears to happen with young men in
their middle and late teens (Figure 5.3). The rise in the
incidence of male suicide, from fifteen to nineteen-year-

49

olds, is quite striking and has also been recognised in other countries.[8] This cannot be due to puberty, which would have occurred several years earlier. However, it may be related to the perception, or non-perception, of unfolding adult roles.

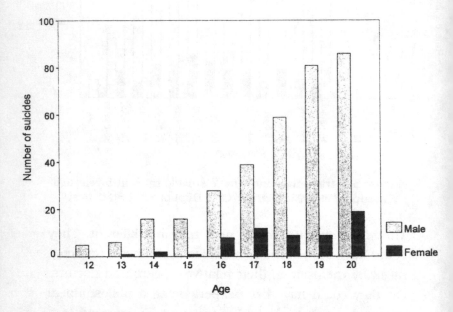

Figure 5.3. Irish male and female suicide by each age up to 20 years, 1976–93. [Source: CSO Dept of Vital Statistics]

It may also relate to the use of alcohol and drugs, as mentioned previously. Alcohol may act as a facilitator of suicide in many young men who are not alcoholics. The importance of drugs as a cause of unnatural deaths has been emphasised in Britain, and regrettably may be becoming an increasingly common cause in Ireland (see Chapter 4).[9]

It is important to state the obvious. Although depression is the most common condition to be associated with suicide, most seriously depressed patients do not end their lives in this way. At most, 10% to 15% of those suffering from deep depression commit suicide.[9] The proportion of alcoholics who ultimately commit suicide is similar to that of the depressed.[10]

Schizophrenia has a similar but somewhat lesser association. One in ten schizophrenic patients end their lives by suicide, and are more likely to do so when well. On the other hand, depressed patients are more likely to do so when ill.[11] For this reason, it is more difficult to predict suicide in schizophrenics. One sufferer, personally known to me, successfully held down an important and demanding job, in spite of his delusive ideas. At Christmas time a few years ago, he got up on the return of his young-adult children after a social night out. Having chatted with them in a perfectly normal and convivial manner, he went out to get cigarettes. He never returned. His car was found by a bridge and his body was found in the river several days later. Chance had played its part in his death. If he had had some cigarettes, or if his children had had some to give him, he would not have had gone out on that fateful night.

Britain has set itself the target of reducing its suicide rate by 15%, by the year 2000. For those known to be psychiatrically ill, it is intended that this drop in suicide be as much as 30%. The Defeat Depression Campaign, jointly run by the Royal College of Psychiatrists and the Royal College of General Practitioners, is essential to this strategy. It was much influenced by a careful, if small

Swedish study on the island of Götland.[12]

This island, with a population of approximately 50,000, had sixteen general practitioners. All but two participated in a detailed educational programme about the recognition and treatment of depression. In the succeeding couple of years the number of suicides fell, although they subsequently rose again. The authors believed that this indicated the need for a 'booster' or follow-up programme. Others, less sanguine, questioned whether the initial fall had been a chance phenomenon, as some years previously the number of suicides was also low. Nevertheless, the study has rightly been hugely influential. Presently, in England, a major study is being planned with a view to testing what the Swedes found, on a much larger population.

Better recognition and better treatment of depression benefit the individual and society. If depression did not exist, it is very likely that the suicide rate would be much lower. The chronic abuse of alcohol and street drugs are also potent causes of suicide. And if this abuse did not occur, the number of suicides would fall even further.

6

SOCIAL DETERMINANTS
OF SUICIDAL BEHAVIOUR

It is true that, on occasion, chance may kill. Genuine suicide, however, always implies intention. Often researchers shy away from this concept on the grounds that one can never be certain of what another intends. However, the establishment of intent is essential in making a formal judgement of suicide. It is believed that many attempters may be ambivalent about the outcome of the event, but set upon a course of action in the knowledge that death is the likely outcome.

With parasuicide, the situation is different. By definition, this refers to any act deliberately undertaken by a patient which mimics the act of suicide, but does not result in death.[1] In some cases the individual does not intend to end his life, but rather to change his circumstances by embarking upon a course of action that could end in death, although very unlikely. Some parasuicidal acts, however, are genuine suicide attempts and such people are more likely to go on to complete the suicide at a later time. The World Health Organisation endeavoured to distinguish between parasuicide and genuine attempts at suicide in 1986.[2] Overall, the proportion of parasuicides who ultimately end their lives by suicide in the subsequent ten to fifteen years, is somewhere between 10% and 15%. This figure is very similar to that for suicide-risk amongst those with deep depression.[1]

No one fully understands the true impact of parasuicidal behaviour; it is likely to be of great cost to the individual, his family, the caring services and society as a whole. It has been thought to be a silly, attention-seeking, self-indulgent form of behaviour, much more common to women than to men. Our research indicates that the reality is different.

In 1982, we examined every case of deliberate self-poisoning admitted to the four casualty departments then serving the city of Cork.[3] The rates of self-poisoning varied hugely across the city (Figure 6.1). The areas of highest deliberate self-poisoning were socially deprived areas – characterised by local-authority housing, unemployment and a high density of people per room and per hectare. These at-risk areas were also characterised by heavy emergency demands on the social services, and a majority of the population had minimum education.

A further study of deliberate self-poisoning in Cork city found that an accurate prediction of an area's self-poisoning rate can be made if one knows the rate of unemployment within the area.[4] Knowing the levels of the other characteristics does not improve the accuracy of the prediction. It is worth noting that it is the incidence of self-poisoning in areas that is being predicted – it is not being claimed that unemployment predicts an individual's act of self-poisoning. The next chapter will delineate the importance of unemployment in individual cases.

It could be argued that these geographical differ-

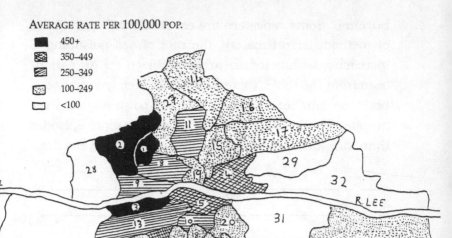

AVERAGE RATE PER 100,000 POP.

- 450+
- 350–449
- 250–349
- 100–249
- <100

Figure 6.1. Incidence of deliberate self-poisoning in Cork city,
1982. [Source: Suicide Research Foundation, Cork]

ences in the rate of self-poisoning simply reflect different
usage of services, according to social class, income and
access to private care. This possibility is presently being
examined. Every general practitioner in Cork city is par-
ticipating in a prospective study of parasuicide, noting
whether the patient is retained within the general practice itself or referred to hospital. An obvious criterion for
referral is the lethality of the act – there is a huge difference between taking 5 tablets and 95 tablets of a given
drug.

Deliberate self-poisoning accounts for between 70%
and 80% of parasuicides; the remainder consisting of
acts of self-cutting, attempted drowning, hanging, and

burning.[1] Some repeaters are consistent in their choice of method. Unfortunately, the rate of self-poisoning is increasing within urban areas (Table 6.1). As can be seen from the table, there has been a steady increase in both the number of episodes of self-poisoning and the number of individuals involved. There are more episodes than individuals, as some individuals repeated the act.

	1982	1988	1992
No. of individuals	243	285	336
No. of episodes	308	316	383

Table 6.1. Number of episodes of self-poisoning and number of individuals involved in Cork city, 1982, 1988 and 1992. [Source: Suicide Research Foundation, Cork]

There have been many reports of social inequalities in health care.[5] Cork is no exception. The general health of individuals living in deprived areas is below average and certainly not ideal. Petty crime and street violence characterise some of these areas. Those who deliver essential services (teachers, doctors, police, etc.) are likely to live elsewhere and only to visit during duty hours. The clergy may still be one exception to this general rule and because of this, they are likely to act as community leaders.

Right across Europe, two very divergent urban-cultures have been developing. One is comfortable, docile and smug; the other is disturbed, deprived and dangerous. In Britain and Northern Ireland, this division is complicated by racial prejudice and religious difference respectively.

This problem may get worse. European money is helping to transform buildings in some city centres. The cost of transforming social structures is likely to be far greater, however, and will require much more ingenuity and resourcefulness.

The west is used to criticising eastern Europe – particularly the Soviet Union during Stalin's regime, on the grounds of the massive enforced transportation of population which he and his administration put into effect. And yet, we think little of the piecemeal urban transportations that were carried out in most cities of Ireland over the past forty or fifty years. Old communities were sundered. Young couples were moved away from their extended families, often severing access to stable role models. Frequently, accommodation was constructed in advance of other necessary services. Housing estates consisting of young, poorly educated parents, with no access to sources of wisdom and experience, were commonplace.

Education can help to resolve these problems. Evidence from Canada suggests that delinquency can be predicted from as young as three years of age.[6] Early intervention, before kindergarten age, prevents the development of antisocial behaviour. Deprived families who receive education while the children are still only infants, do better than those who wait until the child is aged about four or five. Housing people in areas without access to education is disastrous. Most third level institutions have positioned themselves in more salubrious areas. Not only will the poor always be with us, but it would appear that they are always fated to lose out.

7

THE FATE OF SELF-
POISONERS

A follow-up to the 1982 study of self-poisoners in Cork city, was carried out some eight to ten years later. Of the 245 individuals involved in the initial study, 195 were successfully identified and contacted; 99 of these were interviewed face-to-face, for 57 cases a relative was interviewed, and in the remaining 39 cases hospital notes only were examined.[1]

Most of the individuals came from a background of appalling childhood disadvantage. Of the 111 women, 44% had a family history of mental illness, while 30% had a family history of alcoholism (Figure 7.1). In 6% of cases, suicidal behaviour had occurred in the parents. In a further 16%, suicidal behaviour had occurred among other relatives. Of the total, 9% had spent time in care and 15% were the subject of physical abuse. One in ten was a victim of sexual abuse. Almost half described their childhood as being unhappy. A similar proportion described other disadvantages, mainly relating to being 'cheated' out of childhood; for example, having to care for elderly relatives and siblings, or having to work in other ways when they should have been at school.

The men had suffered broadly similar hardship. Of

the 84, 42% of the men had a family history of mental illness, while almost 40% had a family history of alcoholism (Figure 7.2). In 3% of cases, suicidal behaviour

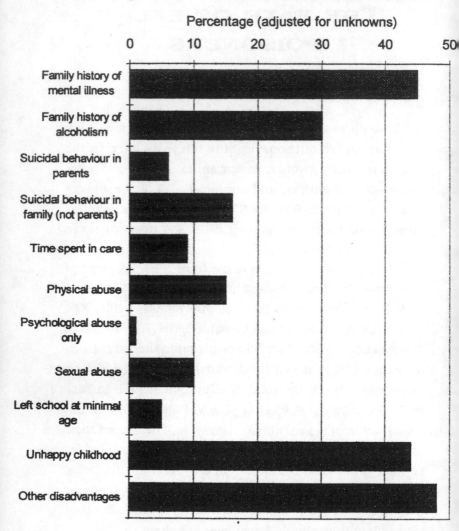

Figure 7.1. Childhood and family disadvantage – females.
[Source: Suicide Research Foundation, Cork]

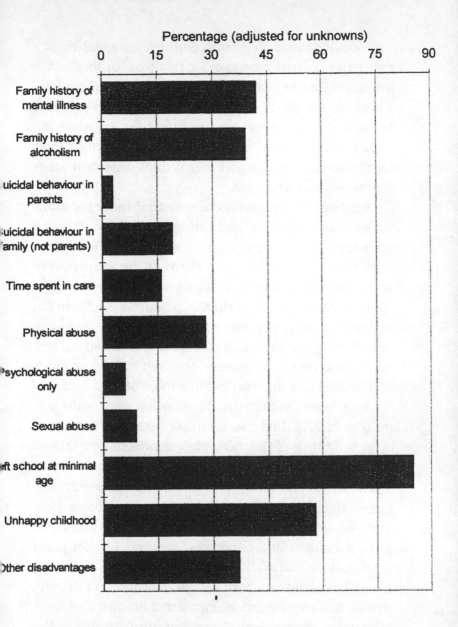

Figure 7.2. Childhood and family disadvantage – males.
[Source: Suicide Research Foundation, Cork]

61

had occurred in the parents. For 19%, suicidal behaviour had occurred among other relatives. In total, 16% had spent time in care, 28% had been subjected to physical abuse and 6% to sexual abuse. As many as 85% had left school at the minimum age, if not earlier, while 9% lacked discipline and training. Over half described their childhood as unhappy and over a third described other significant disadvantages.

Contrary to the traditional view that these individuals were self-indulgent and acting in response to trivial occurrences, most had major difficulties and disabilities at the time of overdose. Two-thirds of the women were psychiatrically ill and 45% had a history of previous psychiatric illness, with a similar proportion suffering a major personality deficiency (Figure 7.3). Over a quarter had current problems with alcohol and 14% had current addictions. Domestic violence occurred in 16% of cases and marital discord occurred in almost 60% of cases.

With regard to the men, the situation was hardly better (Figure 7.4). There was a major personality deficiency in two-thirds of the men, while approximately 60% of the sample were psychiatrically ill at the time of overdose. Almost half had a previous history of psychiatric illness and a similar figure had previously self-poisoned. Three-quarters of the men had current alcohol problems, while a similar number had had previous alcohol problems. A third had addiction problems, mainly to benzodiazepines (drugs such as Valium, Librium and Ativan). Almost half were experiencing marital discord and four-fifths were unemployed. As well as this, a third of the sample had a history of criminality.

62

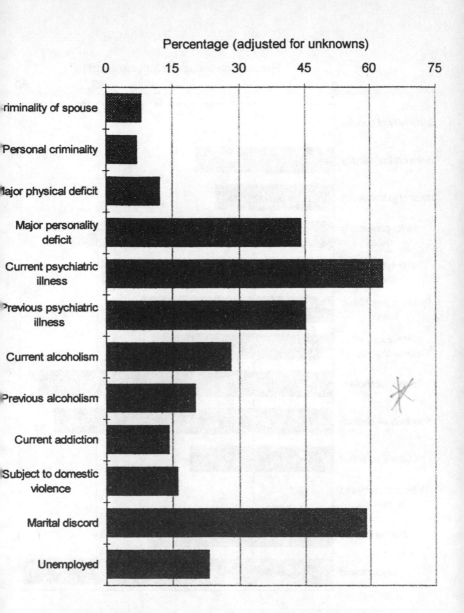

Figure 7.3. Social and personal deficit at time of overdose –
females. [Source: Suicide Research Foundation, Cork]

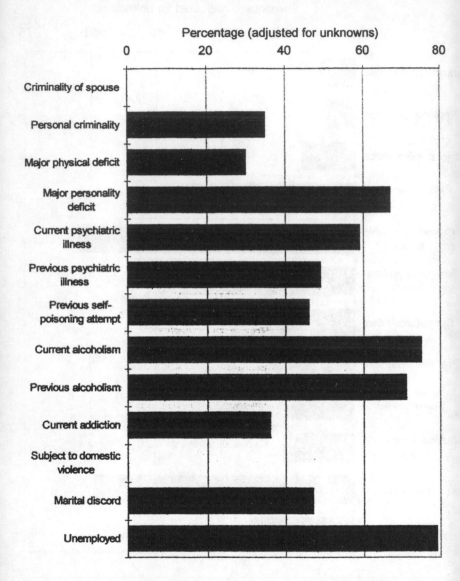

Figure 7.4. Social and personal deficit at time of overdose – males. [Source: Suicide Research Foundation, Cork]

The results of the follow-up study, for both men and women, were abysmal. Over 40% of the women had self-poisoned again during the ten year period, while 12% had engaged in other acts of deliberate self-harm (Figure 7.5). Some 6% had died, several of these by suicide. In the year of follow-up, a third were treated for a psychiatric illness, with just over a third treated for alcoholism and 13% treated for benzodiazepine dependence. Three-quarters of those available for employment were unemployed most of the time. Over a third were thought to be at risk of repeating the self-injurious behaviour.

The situation with respect to the men was even worse (Figure 7.6). Two-thirds had engaged in subsequent acts of self-poisoning and a third had engaged in other acts of deliberate self-harm. Some 13% had died, most of these being unnatural deaths. Almost a third were treated for a psychiatric illness in the follow-up year, while almost two-thirds were treated for alcoholism and over 40% treated for benzodiazepine dependency. Two-thirds of the men had been unemployed for most of the ten years and 11% had spent time in prison. A half were regarded as being at risk of repeating the self-injurious behaviour.

None of this makes for uplifting reading, but it still does not, unfortunately, tell the whole story. Harm to the self is also tinctured with harm to others. No mention is made of the harm to children that such disturbed parents may cause. The fact that the latter were themselves victims of physical, sexual and emotional abuse, does not bode well for their children. Apart from mental illness, the typical response includes abuse of alcohol and

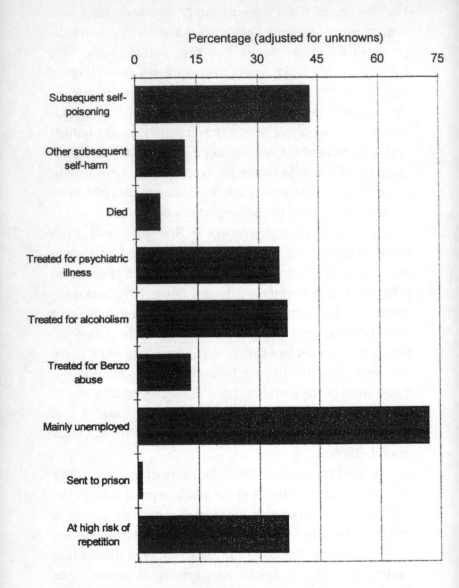

Figure 7.5. Negative aspects of outcome – females. [Source: Suicide Research Foundation, Cork]

drug-dependency.[2] The level of repetition of self-harm is startlingly high, particularly amongst the men. Some of the individuals in the sample fit the mould of the 'grand repeater'.[3] It would appear that deliberate self-poisoning takes on the characteristics of compulsive or addictive behaviour. For some, it may have been an act of frustration against the self; while for others, an attempt to manipulate those around them. It may also have been a way, for a few, to access hospital services. Some may have miscalculated the dosage and died as a result.

Obviously, not all cases had such poor outcomes. One female student who had taken an overdose, recovered and returned to university, where she subsequently received a PhD. Another individual who had self-poisoned also graduated and found work abroad. Unfortunately, these were the exceptions. The majority had more in common with the detritus thrown up by what has been called the cycles of disadvantage.[4] Or in scriptural terms, that 'the sins of the parents will be meted on the children'.

It is easy to be critical of these people, who absorb such a disproportionate amount of health care services. However, they are by and large deprived and know nothing but deprivation. The long term alleviation of the problem may have more to do with education, public health and employment, rather than an emergency clinical response, which is the 'sticking plaster' approach.[5] In good surgical practice one does not suture festering wounds. Prevention is always better than cure.

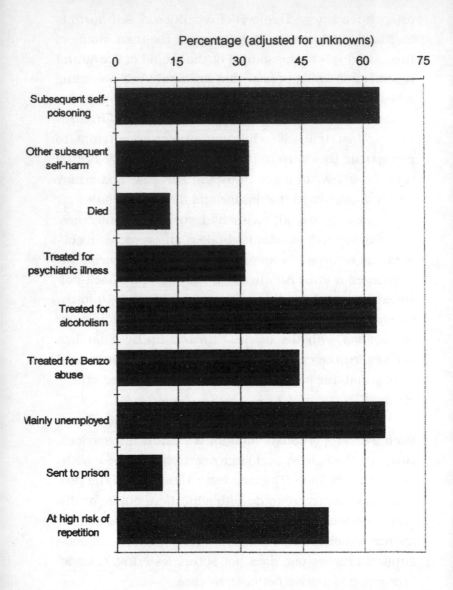

Figure 7.6. Negative aspects of outcome – males. [Source: Suicide Research Foundation, Cork]

8

THE RESPONSE OF FAMILY AND FRIENDS

A study of the Southern Health Board area, done conjointly by the CSO and the coroners, suggested that suicide in Cork and Kerry may be under-estimated by 15% to 20%.[1] If one accepts that the official number of suicides in the Republic of Ireland is approximately 350 per annum, then it is reasonable to assume that the true number is in the order of 410 per annum. Some causes of unnatural death are more difficult than others to classify; for example, medicinal self-poisoning in an elderly person who may be confused, or a drowning when a person may have unwisely gone for a swim. If every individual has, on average, seven relatives spread across the three family generations of children, parents and grandparents; then it may be assumed that, in Ireland, about 3,000 people have to deal directly with the reality of suicide each year. How do the bereaved respond?

Until recently, society dictated that their grief be silent, hidden and full of shame. This is beginning to change. Suicide has been decriminalised and self-help groups have emerged. These groups are endeavouring to organise their own response to suicide loss.

For some of the bereaved, the tragedy begins with an unexpected knock on the door. A garda, a priest, or a doctor may have the unpleasant and stressful task of breaking the news. How one breaks such news is very important. It takes time. It is best not to come out with the whole story at once, but rather, to convey the information step-by-step. Sometimes the person burdened with the task of disclosing the information is not privy to all the facts, as he might not have been a witness to either the death or the discovery. How one communicates bad news, however, can be very important in protecting the future emotional life of the individual.

For others, the body of the deceased may never be discovered. This is even more traumatic. One retired, separated man known to me, scans the faces he passes in the street, in the hope of seeing his only son who has been missing for seven years now. He believes his son is dead, probably drowned. Yet, the searching continues – and because of his marital status, he has no confidant with whom to share his loss.

The worst tragedy, however, is to unexpectedly discover the body oneself. An ambitious mother, known to me through research work done in Britain, discovered her son (who had been attending a prestigious and highly academic London school) hanged in her wardrobe. When seen by me several years after the death, she was still actively grieving. Many other examples come to mind: a school boy finding his father in a smoke-filled car; a school girl who found her father hanged in the garage; frantic parents who found their student son at the bottom of a cliff; siblings who found their professionally-successful brother shot on the living-room floor; and a farmer who came upon his wife drowned in a rainwater barrel.

Most of us never have to face a personal challenge of these proportions. Those of us who have lost relatives who were so much a part of our development that they were almost integrated into our being, know what it is to have them unexpectedly torn away. The response of those who are bereaved by suicide is similar, but there are special difficulties associated with the fact that, here, the deceased had died by choice and by their own hands.

Initially, there may be an interplay of conflicting emotions, with symptoms in keeping with anxiety and depression. For some, the immediate response is one of numbness and shock; in extreme cases, the person may not respond emotionally or verbally at all. Others maintain appropriate social responses, but do so in an automatic way, without inner involvement. Sometimes, such people have little memory afterwards as to how they behaved at the time.[2]

Still others will be conscious of surging feelings of anger that may be directed towards employers, friends, partners, therapists or the deceased themselves. There is often a tremendous sense of guilt – associated with questioning, doubting and criticism of oneself – for not anticipating or responding to whatever had been distressing the deceased.

Confusion is yet another response; not just an uncertainty of time and place, but an inability to make decisions and to organise one's own thoughts. Sometimes there is an effort to deny the death, and to assume or hope that there has been a mistake. More frequently, the supposition of suicide (which involves intention) is disputed. There is a protective drive to demonstrate that the death had been accidental.

Socially, suicide differs from natural death in several ways. Burial is not the end of society's demands: there is the matter of the post-mortem examination which may delay the funeral arrangements; there is the announcement in the newspaper, which may strive to explain the unexpected nature of the death; and there follows an inquest which may not be held for some time, but which keeps alive the possibility that the circumstances of the death will be openly and publicly discussed at some future date. Fortunately, priests, undertakers, doctors and coroners are usually skilled in handling these situations. The bereaved, on the other hand, are generally unfamiliar with the proceedings and may look upon what is to happen with great foreboding.

We are fashioned by nature to overcome grief and loss. Most people, no matter how great the trauma, usually succeed. However, for the sensitive, emotional pain can never be avoided. Some may experience illness, due to distress, in the weeks or months following the suicide of a loved one. The anniversary, Christmas and birthdays may all have a similar effect, as can an unrelated death or even the death of a pet. Each history is different, although the presentation of illness, once it occurs, has universal qualities.

Depression may present with two diverse sets of symptoms. Subjectively, the individual may now see his own future as being hopeless, his world as being meaningless and himself as being worthless. Objectively, his sleep may be disturbed, he may have difficulty in falling asleep, and he may be awakening during the night or early in the morning. Appetite may diminish leading to weight loss, whilst, occasionally, there is recourse to compensatory eating with weight gain. Energy may be low and disinterest common. Socially and occupationally, there is withdrawal.[3]

Anxiety is a sense of dread and apprehension about the future. It is associated with a loss of confidence and a loss of assertiveness. Although, if a person is threatened, he may respond with a vehemence and anger that surprises even himself. There may be a fear of going out, as well as a fear of being alone. Added to this, there is a gnawing fear that the suicide will be imitated – by oneself, as sometimes happens; or by children and siblings, as is more frequently the case.

Depression and anxiety are often mixed. Anger and a need to apportion blame are common experiences. Recourse to alcohol or medicinal drugs (in particular the benzodiazepines, which are commonly prescribed for both anxiety and sleep), is a further hazard.

The individual's future emotional and psychological health will be determined by how he or she responds to these unforeseen stresses. It is important to emphasise that it is natural to feel pain. In a sense, emotional pain helps to cleanse our minds, at least initially. Such pain must be faced and cannot be avoided. Yet, we have a responsibility to ourselves, our families and society, to rise above and move on from the trauma. The aim is not to forget the deceased and the manner of his death; but rather to remember him as he was, before the pain and distress caused by his parting.

Some emotionally resourceful people have a capacity to talk themselves through a problem. Most, however, benefit from having a spouse, friend or close relative with whom they can share their troubles. Time and effort bring release from self-criticism and blame. It is important to gradually re-establish the social routine of one's life. Each of us has a public-self and a private or inner-self – for the secure, these two perceptions of the self are intimately bonded together. However, distress and loss may temporarily sever this connection. The work of personal rehabilitation demands the putting together of these two aspects of the self; so that one's integration is automatic and not consciously contrived, spontaneous and not forced.

Many of those bereaved by suicide have found psychological and social support through the good offices of the Friends of the Suicide Bereaved (see end of chapter for details). It is important that such voluntary organisations remain independent of the statutory and professional services. One is of assistance to the other – much as Alcoholics Anonymous has learned to co-operate with professional services and other voluntary organisations over the years. No one person and no one organisation encompasses the whole truth. The professional has his books and his clinical and research experience. The bereaved have their own searing understanding, clarified and refined in the furnace of conflicting emotional loss.

Parasuicide is not the same – there is no death. The intention may have been to change life circumstances, rather than to end life. Some acts of parasuicide are genuine suicide attempts. Such persons require close observation and specialist treatment. Usually the death-wish vanishes as the illness improves, but this may not always be so.

Relatives of parasuicides are faced with difficult problems. The attempt, no matter how trivial, should never be ignored. Assessment by a professional, experienced in such assessments, is essential. The mental attitude of the attempter must be explored in a detailed manner, and further consultation may be necessary to assess progress.

No one knows the full extent of the stress put upon relatives by those exhibiting suicidal behaviour. It is essential to understand the cause of such behaviour: sometimes it is due to illness; sometimes it may be related to alcohol or drugs; while, most frequently, it is a response to perceived distressing circumstances. Often, the relative who accompanies the patient to hospital is construed by the individual as being the source of his anguish.

The challenge for the relative and the attempter is to re-order their relationship and their domestic situations. The challenge for the professional is to prevent recurrence, which (as outlined in the previous chapter) is surprisingly common. Unfortunately, however, prevention of suicidal behaviour is a difficult matter. If it were easy, there would be no need or place for research into suicide and parasuicide.[3]

As discussed previously, the stress of the suicide-bereaved, or of those affected by parasuicide, occasionally reaches illness proportions, requiring medical treatment.[2] The best person to consult is a general practitioner whom one knows and trusts. He may treat the person himself, or refer them to a clinical psychologist or psychiatrist. The difference between these two specialists, is that the latter is medically qualified and, as such, can diagnose illness and prescribe medicines. Both can act as psychotherapists, although the approach may vary. If it is an emergency and the person does not have a general practitioner, they may present themselves at their local psychiatric hospital and see a consultant, without a referral letter. Many psychiatric units now have services available in the casualty departments of local general hospitals.

9

PREVENTION AT NATIONAL LEVEL

In November 1995, the Minister of Health, Michael Noonan TD, announced the setting up of a task force on suicide, following consultation with Senator Dan Neville and myself. This task force is to examine the problem of suicide and parasuicide, and to make recommendations as to how the upward trends might be reversed. An understanding as to how diverse the problem of suicidal behaviour is, may be gathered from a brief review of the backgrounds of those invited to become members of the task force.

There are to be two directors of public health, in recognition of the fact that suicide is much wider than clinical medicine. The greatest advance in the health and well-being of our communities over the past one hundred years, has had much more to do with housing, adequate diet, clean water and clean air, than it has to do with the discovery of antibiotics or other medical and technological progress. As has already been shown (Chapters 6 and 7), parasuicide is largely a public health issue, although it is the casualty departments of general hospitals that deal with the consequences of most attempts.[1, 2]

Most suicides occur amongst the mentally ill. Previous admission to a psychiatric hospital is a predictor of suicide in an individual, although of low magnitude. Several studies have shown that in the weeks following discharge from psychiatric hospitals, people are particularly vulnerable to suicide.[3] Hence the importance of putting the Inspector of Mental Hospitals on the committee. One should not be surprised that suicide has an association with mental hospitals, for the simple reason that the most vulnerable are attracted and referred there. If one were studying sudden death due to heart disease, one would find the highest incidence among those seeking admission, already admitted, or recently discharged from specialist cardiac units. The same applies to suicide and specialist psychiatric departments.

Suicide was decriminalised in Ireland in 1993. Up until then, it had been a crime to either attempt or complete suicide. Legislative attempts to change the law were not without political incident.[4] During the nineteenth century, suicide attempters were imprisoned in the belief that if specialist chaplains could counsel them there, repetition would be avoided.[5] Since then, the Department of Justice has always been involved in both suicides and attempted suicides. Its interest in suicide will remain, because all cases of unnatural death must be adjudged by the coroners, and because the police continue to investigate such deaths and make a confidential report to the CSO. For this reason, a senior garda officer and a coroner were invited to join the committee.

The Samaritans is the largest voluntary organisation in the country offering non-directive, supportive counselling to the distressed – therefore, it was appropriate that an experienced member of the organisation be invited to join.[6] Many of those bereaved by suicide, or those who engage in acts of parasuicide, seek counselling – hence the appointment of a psychologist. And, since most cases of parasuicide are referred to casualty, a hospital administrator was selected as a member.[7] A psychiatrist with a strong background of research in the area was appointed, in recognition of the fact that progress will not be made without strict definition of the problem and careful examination of novel means of intervention. And finally, a senior civil servant with a background in health education was given chairmanship of the group.

The Irish constitution is a very paternalistic one: it focuses on the family and makes reference to treating all the nation's children equally.[8] In a sense, as far as the constitution is concerned, we are all children. Many families bereaved by suicide are reassured when they accept that everything they could do as parents and siblings, was done – even if their relative took his own life. We should adopt the same attitude nationally. Suicide, like poverty and illness, may always be with us. We have a responsibility, individually and collectively, to keep the numbers as low as is humanly feasible. The overall function of the task-force will be to see that we are doing just this.

This immediately raises the question as to whether suicide is actually preventable. A fatalist would answer no; his argument being, that if someone is intent on killing himself, nothing is going to stop him. This argument is flawed. Most people who make a serious attempt on their lives, once treated and having recovered, do not kill themselves later. As mentioned previously (Chapter 6), about 10% to 15% of the parasuicidal referred to casualty, go on to commit suicide in the succeeding ten to fifteen years.[9] In other words, 85% to 90% of parasuicides avoid suicide. Hence the fallacy of fatalism. The challenge is, however, how to better these figures.

Scientists have always grappled with the notion of human choice and the implications of free will. Choice is equated with unpredictability. It is often the case that predictions and hypotheses can be made on an overall basis, but not on an individual one. This is the case with suicide. However, as stated earlier (Chapter 4), road traffic accidents have decreased, even though human error (and thereby choice) is the most significant contributory factor.[10] Furthermore, choice is always open to persuasion. There is a whole industry of public relations which rests on this belief. In general terms, suicide should be no different.

For some suicides, the mind changes in the hours or days before death. It is likely that the main change is in selective attention and inattention. The focus of the mind narrows. Only the problem is seen, with no solution other than death in sight. To an outsider, the distress may appear transient. Suicide as an outcome, however, is permanent. The blinkered view of the suicidal person prevents them from seeing other solutions to their problems. Some suicides are selfish and do not consider the consequences for others. The bereaved may be left to face the same problems, alone. Sometimes the suicide intends not only to end his life, but also to hurt someone close to him. In more cases, little consideration is given to the self or to others; death is on impulse rather than design.

In the nineteenth century, moral persuasion was the main method used to respond to suicide attempts.[5] Durkheim, who was a social optimist, believed that society would reform itself – somewhat like the old guild system, whereby religion would be replaced by a new set of meaningful relationships and purposes, leading to a containment or fall in suicide.[11] The twentieth century has been characterised by faith in medicines and medical practice. Despite better training of doctors, the availability of effective medications and the growth of many voluntary, protective organisations such as The Samaritans; suicide rates have not fallen.[9]

Recent work suggests that we should tackle the problem of suicide in much the same way as we have successfully done for accidents, basing our approach on earlier work done on the principles of accident prevention.[12, 13, 14]

These principles are threefold, the first being to get people to alter behaviour that puts them at risk.[15] In terms of suicide prevention, this means persuading people to drink less and with particular caution when stressed; further strengthening the fight against street drugs; and teaching people, especially the young, that it is not shameful to confide distress.

The second principle is to improve on existing laws with a view to preventing accidents. In relation to suicide prevention: changing prescribing habits so that repeat-prescriptions would be unlawful; limiting the sale of potentially harmful medicinal substances to particular outlets; limiting the quantities of drugs that one may purchase by selling them in blister packs only; and being more stringent in the issuing of gun licences, including the insistence that the licensee sign a statement that ammunition will always be kept separately to the gun.

The final principle is to prevent accidents by altering the environment appropriately. In terms of suicide: to limit access to roofs of tall buildings, stairwells and notorious bridges; to restrict the use of coal-gas for domestic consumption, when the less toxic natural gas is available; to introduce an automatic-door system on trains, which limits access to the railway line (such as they have in Japan and as are now being introduced in London); to modify cars by the inclusion of catalytic converters, thereby reducing the toxicity of the exhaust fumes (which apart from preventing suicide, would be kinder to the environment); to reshape the end of ex-haust pipes, so that a hose pipe could not be easily attached; and lastly, to install a sensor within the car that disconnects the power should the carbon monoxide levels increase beyond a minimum point.

There are risks associated with suicide prevention. Sometimes well-intended acts do not produce the desired effect. The media has been shown to wield a greatly beneficial influence, but also, on occasion, a very damaging one.[16] Reporting trends is important. The newsworld has made it plain that something has to be done about the problem of self-inflicted deaths. Many newspapers have published informed articles and written editorials recommending action. Radio has also actively addressed the problem, as has television, although to a lesser extent. The reporting of individual suicides, however, may be dangerous.[17]

In the United States, it has been estimated that one in five suicides is copy-cat.[15] Most people now accept the potential harm that may be caused by media-reported suicides.[16] Some authors have gone so far as to suggest that there is a relationship between the 'dose of publicity' and the likelihood of imitation. In other words, the greater the amount and frequency of coverage given to individual suicides, the more likely it is that the vulnerable young will follow a similar course of action. Older people and the less vulnerable are not as much at risk. Dramatising the event or making a hero of the deceased may be dangerous. Banner headlines on the front page of a Sunday newspaper and showing the picture of fellow students carrying the coffin of a young suicide, during the course of the Leaving Certificate in 1995, may have had lethal consequences for others. It is fallacious to suggest that common stresses, such as the sitting of examinations, are in themselves causes of rare events such as suicide.

Suicide awareness programmes aimed at the young have also provoked controversy in many countries, including the United States and Canada. The controversy surrounding these programmes centres on whether they are beneficial or actually harmful. Those who favour such programmes are often sensitive to criticism, which they take personally. In fact, whereas no one doubts the good intentions, good effects are hard to demonstrate. One renowned researcher insists that these school programmes have negative effects.[17]

Instead, it is recommended that the vulnerable be identified and referred for appropriate professional care. It goes without saying, however, that our schooling (particularly of boys) should be broadened to encompass emotional as well as intellectual development. Intelligence may help the student through the academic gateways in his path. However, personality governs well-rounded success. Better treatment of illness – particularly depression – is essential if suicide is to be contained and reduced in frequency. This may include long term supportive psychotherapy, as well as the use of medications. Britain has focused on this approach, seeking to defeat depression and to enhance suicide prevention among the psychiatrically ill in general.[18]

The Suicide Research Foundation is presently developing three approaches to the management of parasuicide. In one of these, suitable patients are given special cognitive skills training in problem-solving, with a view to assisting them in the choice of positive action should they become stressed at a future date.[19] Secondly, those who are vulnerable are being provided with a pocket card that gives information on services they may require. This means that the individual can have more control over their own care, without resorting to deliberate self-harm in an effort to get professional attention.[20] And finally, statistical and clinical methods of predicting the likelihood of recurrence are being developed, so that those most at risk will be given appropriate support.

In some cases there may be a biological basis to suicide, associated with, or perhaps independent of, the

84

biochemical basis of depression. Serotonin, as already stated (Chapter 4), is a widely distributed brain neurotransmitter, of importance in inhibiting many neuronal pathways and circuits. Studies have shown that those who are impulsively aggressive, have abnormal responses to serotonin.[21] If such people could be identified in advance, it might be possible to predict and prevent suicidal acts. The Suicide Research Foundation is presently examining this possibility.[22, 23]

It used to be thought that immunology was a discreet body function, unconnected with our brains and minds. The opposite is the case. It has been shown that there may be immunological changes in those who make suicide attempts.[24] It is important that these relationships be clarified. This also forms a part of our current work.

Research is essential to the understanding and management of suicide and attempted suicide. It is no longer appropriate that we simply import research findings from other countries. We must instead identify our own problems and find our own solutions. It may be correct to say that truth, in particular scientific truth, is nearly always universal. Nevertheless, there are local social and cultural circumstances that influence the prevalence and applicability of research findings. Furthermore, research is a game with standards that vary between countries and cultural groups. As in football and athletics, we should endeavour to play at the optimum level. We can only do that if we see ourselves as competitors with the world's best.

10

HELPING THE SUICIDAL

There appears to be a continuum in relation to suicide; ranging from suicidal ideas on one end, to suicide on the other, with suicidal impulses and attempts in between. Such a simplistic notion may not hold, however. No one knows what the protective and risk factors are that act as gateways between these four groupings. Furthermore, a person may jump from one end of the spectrum to the other, without passing through the intervening two stages.

We are certain, however, that transient suicidal ideas are relatively common among the young.[1] Most people who entertain suicidal ideas, however briefly, do not advance to a compulsion to do it. Also, most of those with suicidal impulses never actually make an attempt on their lives. As has been explained several times in earlier chapters of this book, the majority of attempters never complete the act of suicide. These points are emphasised because nothing is to be gained by increasing the anxiety of either the individual, or society itself. Moreover, there is a danger of implanting negative ideas in the minds of the young (as may happen in suicide awareness programmes), as well as affirming suicidal intention in someone exposed to suicidal impulse.[2] The Pied Piper has many guises. The impressionable easily follow and may fulfil ill-considered prophecies, if unwittingly given.

On the other hand, none of these dimensions should be ignored – either by the individual, his relatives, his teachers, his work-mates or friends. They must be put into the open and assessed for what they are. We have a responsibility to preserve life, including that of ourselves. The ethics of these matters will be considered in the next chapter.

It is, however, incorrect to say that those who talk about committing suicide never do so. The truth is, that most of those who die by suicide have given signals and hints of varying clarity before they come to their end.[3] Regrettably, the significance of statements is not always clear until death has occurred. One person, known to me, was given to making statements as to how people would feel if and when she were gone. She bought Christmas presents early one particular year, remembered her godchild's birthday well in advance and made the PIN of her bank account known to her family – before she was found hanging by her grandmother's grave. She had never been treated.

Most women, however, who die by suicide have received treatment.[4] The one hundred Irish suicides examined by the Suicide Research Foundation (chapters 1 & 5), showed that 80% of the women had been treated prior to their deaths. A cynic might argue that this had not done them much good. A realist might reply that the fact that so many were treated, might explain why the female suicide rate is so much lower than that of the male.

Half of the men in the sample had not received any known treatment in the year before their deaths. The figure is even more striking and upsetting for the young. Of the 15–24 year-old males, only one in five had received treatment. The rest went to their graves without even the chance of therapy.

The message here is clear. Do not ignore suicidal impulses, ideas, or attempts – in yourself or in others known to you. Be open, both with yourself and with those whom you can personally trust. A trusting relationship is essential to our psychological well-being. It is not good for man to be alone. We all prosper emotionally by developing human relationships. Such relationships protect against suicide.[5]

If (on reflection or through conversation with a trusted friend or relative) it is thought that further help is necessary; such help is readily available. Those eligible for medical cards can have a consultation with a general practitioner, free of charge. Otherwise, one usually has to pay whatever therapist one employs. Any person, however, may present themselves at a psychiatric hospital and request a consultation. There is a statutory obligation to deliver it. The structure of the psychiatric health service has changed in recent years and further change is planned. The intention is to deliver the service as close to the patient's home as is practically feasible, and furthermore, to provide this service within a general hospital, where stigma is less likely to attach.

The psychiatric health service is divided into catchment areas of, on average, 100,000 people, or thereabouts. Some rural catchment areas are smaller and some urban ones larger. These catchment areas are fur-ther divided into sectors, which have treatment teams (made up of a consultant psychiatrist, a psychologist, a social worker and nurses trained as therapists). Access to the service is usually through a general practitioner or through the casualty department of a general hospital.

An initial assessment is carried out by a qualified and fully-registered doctor, who is either trained in psy-chiatry or in the process of being trained. This doctor is, in turn, responsible to a consultant through the offices of a registrar or senior registrar. Ultimately, the consul-tant is responsible for the clinical practice of his or her juniors. All of this is emphasised because we live in a time when many set themselves up as therapists, with-out registered or supervised training.

This is not to deny that the greatest asset a success-ful therapist has, is his or her personality. The therapist must have come to terms with his own anxieties and must have established his own commitment to life itself, complete with its varied potentialities. A patient who is ambivalent about continuing his life, is not likely to be helped by someone who shares the same ambivalence. Good humour, a light touch and appropriate laughter – even in the face of death – are rarely lost. Skill and exper-tise are the bedfellows of common sense.

Psychiatrists are not the only professionals with spe-cialised knowledge of mental and behavioural problems. Psychologists undergo a different training, both at undergraduate and postgraduate level. Professional rivalry is not uncommon. It may in fact benefit the ser-vice. Some general practitioners and members of the public prefer direct referral to psychologists. The important thing is that a problem should be professionally addressed. If one approach is not working – whether psychological or psychiatric – either switch to another therapist within the same field or try a different approach. The best therapists of either field, however, have much more in common with each other than with other members of the same field.

Voluntary organisations may be of great benefit and assistance to the lonely, anxious and depressed. A list of telephone numbers of some of these voluntary services is given at the end of this chapter.

The Samaritans are the most widely distributed voluntary group. For the price of a local call, they can be contacted from anywhere in Ireland. Confidentiality is guaranteed and face-to-face interview can be arranged. They are widely and frequently used. About 20% of their calls are suicide-related, the rest being from those seeking assuagement of loneliness and distress.

GROW is a self-help group organised by those with mental health problems. It provides a system of group therapy in which the individual is encouraged to come to terms with his feelings of distress, and to use the group dynamic to attain agreed goals within his own life. Many find it of benefit. Its founder had two sets of problems: one relating to alcohol and which he conquered through Alcoholics Anonymous; the other relating to a mood-disorder, which was adequately and appropriately treated within hospital. He found, however, that upon discharge, support structures were inadequate. He developed his own system, using the AA as an initial model. It is not necessary to have had an illness treated in hospital to become a member. Anyone can join, after peer consultation.

AWARE is a self-help group where the leaders or facilitators are specially trained. In the past, they have tended to be professionals – frequently psychiatric nurses. There are groups for both patients and relatives. All the patients have attended doctors and most may be receiving medicines. Compliance in taking the medication (in the recommended manner) is encouraged, as it is not infrequent for illness relapse to occur in those who default on their medication.

Recovery Incorporated (Ireland area) is another self-help group, based in Chicago. Like the previous two, it has a programme and a set of literature tailored to patient need. It operates throughout Ireland, seven days a week.

The Schizophrenia Association looks after the needs of sufferers and their relatives.

Out-and-About offers services to the phobic.

Alcoholics Anonymous has branches throughout the country. Next to depression, alcohol problems have the most common association with suicidal behaviour.[6] This well-known organisation uses a method based on the disease model of alcoholism. The regular meetings and system of befriending provide a support network for those caught in a cycle of abuse.

Narcotics Anonymous is a self-help group for drug users which operates on the same principles as AA.

The Friends of the Suicide Bereaved offer support at an individual and at a group level. They are developing

91

their own approach to care, including the provision of group leaders.

All of the above voluntary groups compete for funding, either through individual subscription or through the health boards. Lottery monies are frequently provided to such groups.

Not every voluntary service suits everyone. Some may use a service for a time and then move on. For others, it becomes a way of life. The same, of course, happens with professional and hospital services. A Christmas pantomime in Cork once depicted an out-patients' department, where 'the regulars' were engaged in animated conversation. They then realised that a frequent attender was missing. A know-all, however, opined that her absence was probably due to unexpected illness!

Help comes in many shapes and forms. Honesty with oneself is essential to successful therapy. If in doubt, or if distressed, talk to someone. There are many out there, both voluntary and professional, who are very willing to assist.

LIST OF VOLUNTARY SUPPORT ORGANISATIONS:

GROW
(Dublin Office)
167 Capel Street,
Dublin 1
Tel.: 01–8734029

(Cork Office)
11 Liberty Street,
Cork
Tel.: 021–277520

AWARE

(Dublin Office)
147 Phibsborough Road,
Dublin 7
Tel.: 01–6791711

(Cork Office)
Grove House
St. Mary's Orthopaedic Hospital, Cork
Tel.: 021–303264

Alcoholics Anonymous

(Dublin Office)
109 South Circular Road,
Dublin 8
Tel.: 01–4538998

(Cork Office)
Basement Flat,
12A Patrick's Hill,
Cork
Tel.: 021–500481

Narcotics Anonymous

(Dublin Office)
Tel.: 01–8300944

(Cork Office)
Tel.: 021–278411

Recovery Incorporated (Ireland area)

(Dublin Office)
PO Box No. 2210
Dublin 8
Tel.: 01–4535633

(Cork Office)
Blackpool Community Centre
Great William O'Brien Street,
Cork
Tel.: 021–501787

Schizophrenia Association of Ireland
(Dublin Office)
4, Fitzwilliam Place
Dublin 4
Tel.: 01–2954004

Out-and-About
(Dublin Office)
20 St Stephen's Street Lower,
Dublin 2
Tel.: 01–4755066

(Cork Office)
24a Paul Street,
Cork
Tel.: 021–271432

Friends of the Suicide Bereaved
(Cork Office)
PO Box 162,
Cork
Tel.: 021–294318

The Samaritans
(Dublin Office)
112 Marlboro Street,
Dublin 1
Tel.: 01–8727700

(Cork Office)
Coach Street,
Cork
Tel.: 021–271323

Area help line
Tel.: 1850–609090

11

THE MORALITY OF SUICIDE, ASSISTED SUICIDE AND EUTHANASIA

When I first began this work with the late Dr Maura Daly in 1982, I took it for granted that to intentionally end one's life was immoral. That is how I was reared to think. As a doctor, however, one is trained to separate the person from his actions. Convicted criminals and prisoners of war are entitled to the same standards of professional medical care as anyone else. As a psychiatrist, one sometimes sees people whose behaviour is alien to one's own perspective. Yet, insofar as they are ill, they are given the benefit of the skills of the profession.

As previously mentioned, suicide and attempted suicide were decriminalised in Ireland in 1993. It remains a crime, however, to assist someone in killing himself. This is not so in all countries. In Germany, a doctor may advise a patient on a lethal drug dosage and then prescribe such medication, although the physician cannot be present when the patient ingests the drug and dies. In Holland, the doctor may lawfully administer an overdose, provided that certain criteria are fulfilled, including reporting of the matter to the appropriate authorities.[1]

Such behaviour is illegal in Britain and Ireland and in most of the rest of the world. Although, moves are afoot in the United States and Australia to change the law to allow professional assistance in suicide in their countries too.

Over the last decade, several books have been written (particularly in the United States) carrying advice and instructions as to how one might go about ending one's life. More recently, such information has become available on the Internet. Due to this, Befrienders International has distributed their own counter-information through the Internet. Such conflicting viewpoints challenge the security of one's own position. On what do we base the view that suicide is either moral or immoral?

Some might argue that suicide, like death itself, is amoral. The ethics of the event depend on its circumstances and consequences for others and the self. There must be a difference between the suicide of a young man in his prime, and that of a much older man suffering a painful and ultimately fatal illness. Those who say that suicide is always wrong, have difficulty in explaining the deaths of Wolfe Tone (who cut his throat rather than face the indignity of execution) and Terence MacSwiney (who starved himself to death in protest against political injustice).[2]

The English faced the same moral dilemma in 1822, when Lord Castlereagh (no friend of Ireland or Wolfe Tone) cut his throat, presumably in association with a depressive illness.[3] What he did was criminal according to English law of the time. Nevertheless, political shuffling at the highest level accorded him the grandeur of a

state funeral. Church law decreed that he was not entitled to burial in the sanctified grounds of Westminster
cemetery. Under civil law, his property should have been
forfeited to the state – however, this did not happen.

The Old Testament is regarded as a holy book by
Jews, Christians and Muslims. It is believed to be the
word of God, spoken through the prophets. Yet, nowhere
in the Old Testament is suicide condemned. Self-inflicted death is described in a factual way, relating the
method used and the situation where the death occurred. There is never any judgement made.[4]

The New Testament only mentions one suicide; that
of Judas Iscariot, who hanged himself. The implication is
that he had felt so guilty about betraying Jesus to his
captors, he ended his own life. Later Christian writers
maintain that his suicide was a more heinous crime
than the betrayal of Jesus.

The Church's attitude to suicide only really developed around the time of St Augustine (354–430AD).[5]
Much had happened before then, however, to influence
the saint's approach. The mass suicide of Masada had
provoked much thought on the morality of such an act,
especially among the Jews themselves. The teaching of
the Talmud evolved along lines that anticipated later
Christian teaching. The rites of burial of a suicide were
different and less dignified than those received by a non-
suicide. However, if the suicide were of unsound mind,
exceptions were made. In order to be reprehensible, the
act of suicide had to have been voluntary and premeditated. Suicide on impulse was treated lightly. Jewish tradition, however, differed from Christian tradition, in that

it openly stated that some suicides were praiseworthy; for example, self-inflicted death in order to escape forced religious conversion or capture by heathens.[6]

The Stoics – who were very influential socially and philosophically, both in ancient Greece and later in Rome – also regarded such suicides as praiseworthy. Seneca bled himself to death in a bath surrounded by his disciples. The Romans, however, saw suicide among soldiers and slaves as a loss to the workforce and economy. The families of soldiers who committed suicide were deprived of their property. Attempted suicide, either by soldiers or slaves, was punished. It is probable that the frequency of suicide was higher among the non-Christian gentiles than amongst the Christians themselves.

Martyrdom was lauded as a guarantee of immediate entry to heaven, once death had occurred. Tertullian (160–225AD) was fascinated with voluntary death.[7] However, one had an obligation to protect the body, which was construed as being the temple of the Holy Ghost. Provoking the civil authorities in order to achieve martyrdom was less meritorious and possibly sinful. Once Christianity had become the state religion, with the conversion of Constantine (280–337AD), the *raison d'être* of martyrdom disappeared forever. It did not stop the zealots, however. The Donatists developed the idea of voluntary death further; for them, sin was inevitable and salvation could be attained through confession and communion, followed by self-destruction and the direct entry into heaven.[8]

The history of the Donatist variety of Christianity is complicated. Their first bishop, Donatus, had been elected to the metropolitan sea of Carthage about 85 years before Augustine's enthronement at Hippo.[9] Donatus and his followers believed that the incumbent bishop of Carthage and his predecessor had sullied themselves in the last serious religious persecution, by discontinuing public worship. There developed, as a result, two major Christian Churches in North Africa: the Catholic Church in communion with Rome; and the Donatist Church, fiercely independent and believing themselves to be spiritually superior.

Once Christianity became the official state religion, the emperor wanted the Donatists suppressed. A Church council was called, with Augustine present, under a lay imperial chairman. The Donatists attended, but refused to sit down with the 'ungodly'. The council then resolved to exile the Donatist clergy, impose gradated fines and to confiscate their Church property. In effect, they were to be forcibly converted to Catholicism. It was in that context that they set about killing themselves, following sacramental purification. The Jews did the same at York in 1190, when they chose mass suicide in preference to coerced conversion to Christianity.

St Augustine did not stop there, however. He believed and taught the doctrine that human life, as manifested in the individual, was the gift of God. God commanded us not to kill. This Commandment referred to all human life, including the self. What Augustine proposed, as a response to a local situation at a particular time in history, soon became the universal law of the Christian Church.[10] St Thomas Aquinas affirmed Augustine's position. The civil law laid claim to the property of all suicides, not just that of soldiers. Today, insurance companies sometimes retain what ought to be the lawful estate of the insured deceased.

Since the first century, Jewish thought had endeavoured to specify situations where suicide was acceptable or even praiseworthy, as well as the many more frequent situations where it was regarded as evil. The Christian Church, as a struggling minority, glorified martyrdom – provided that the individual did not set out to provoke his own death. The civil authorities turned a blind eye to suicide, except in the case of soldiers and slaves (as discussed earlier in this chapter). Judaism, Christianity and Islam ultimately espoused similar doctrines and practices with regard to the perceived immorality of premeditated, voluntary death.

Kant, a philosopher, believed that suicide was immoral; that one had an obligation to what one would like to see as a universal rule or law, and that if everyone committed suicide, human life would cease.[11] The English philosopher, David Hume, favoured suicide in the event of life becoming too burdensome. He argued that the individual owned his own life and therefore what he did with it was his own business, provided others were not harmed.[12] Many are harmed, however. Some may imitate the act, some may have to continue work left behind and still others may grieve desolately. We are all emotionally, socially and intellectually interdependent. The suicide of one person affects the well-being of another.

As well as relationships with God and fellow man, morality must also consider one's relationship with oneself. For some, life is like a biography; the writer is not simply concerned with what has been done to date, but also with the unfolding future. One cannot complete the biography if one's existence comes to an end before time.[13] This argument suggests that the wrongfulness of suicide may, in part, be related to the amount of enjoyable or useful life left to run. Clearly, the strongest arguments against suicide are mustered by the teachers of the great religions of the western world and Middle East. It is understandable, therefore, that the faithful have lower rates of suicide than those of little or no faith.

Euthanasia actually means 'a good death'. As such, everyone wishes euthanasia on themselves. The word has been coined, however, to mean the act of assisting somebody else in bringing their death forward in time. There are broadly two types of euthanasia: one is voluntary, where the individual requests assistance in ending his life; the other is involuntary, where the decision to end one's life is made by another person on one's behalf. As previously mentioned, doctors in Holland can quite legally practise euthanasia once they fulfil certain obligations when carrying out such an act. It is noteworthy that Holland, a country with well-developed social services, has little or no hospice care.

The great danger of euthanasia is that it may be seen as a way of saving money. It has been estimated that in the United States, a third of the health-care budget is spent on those in the last six months of life. If euthanasia were legalised – particularly involuntary euthanasia – there might be pressure to increasingly shorten this 'hopeless period'.[15] This happened in Germany fifty years ago, in the case of the mentally ill. It may happen again, both in Europe and elsewhere, if the activists who favour it succeed.

12

THE SUICIDE OF PAT TIERNEY

Throughout this book I have avoided identifying particular individuals, apart from those of historical importance. Pat Tierney is an exception. He identified himself as a suicide in an unusual way. A few days before he hanged himself in a churchyard, on his thirty-ninth birthday, he contacted Brenda Power of the *Sunday Tribune* and told her of his plans in a matter-of-fact manner. Some months previously, he had made a similar confession to a friend, but the friend informed a doctor soon after he had made two attempts on his life.

He was furious at what he regarded as a breach of trust. He was taken to the casualty department of St Vincent's Hospital and subsequently transferred, compulsorily, to St Brendan's Psychiatric Hospital, Dublin. Throughout, he was a reluctant patient. He sought his freedom and he retained his desire to die.

He hated the Catholic Church with a vengeance. He regarded their stories of the Holy Family as a sick joke. He himself desired, although never experienced, an emotionally sustaining life. The lack of caring and bonding in his early years was probably instrumental in preventing him from developing sound, persisting, interpersonal relationships. His intelligence did not compensate for the emotional devastation of his childhood.

He wrote a direct, telling, honest and engrossing book, entitled *The Moon on My Back*.[1] The *Sunday Tribune* reported his final conversation with the journalist Brenda Power on 7 January 1996, and she further discussed her moral dilemma on RTE radio's *This Week* the same day.[2] The *Irish Times* subsequently contacted me at home, requesting that I write an article for the newspaper, published on Monday, 8 January 1996. The following is what I said, taken from the newspaper:

Pat Tierney attempted suicide twice. On the second occasion he was successful. After the first attempt he was admitted to a mental hospital.

This in itself is not an unusual story. What is unusual is the different responses of the people he told and the manner in which his 'suicide note' was published. Locked into these communications is a moral dilemma that we in Ireland may yet have to face.

Those who knew Pat (I did not, but I did listen to him reciting poetry on Grafton Street), will remember him as an articulate, well-spoken young man, whose ability far outstripped his formal education.

He rose above every conceivable deprivation – maternal rejection, institutional care, child abuse, living rough as a teenager, petty crime, life as a vagrant worker in the US, drug dependence, broken heterosexual relationships and finally, the uncertainty of advancing AIDS contracted from a dirty needle.

Yet he chose to end his life and to make a public and well-publicised statement in doing so. That was his wish.

It is likely that he sought through his public persona what he did not have and never experienced as a child – love, respect and a sense of emotionally shared vision of future unfolding adult life.

Public recitation of poetry, the writing of verse, the production of his play and the publication of his autobiography may, at least in part, have been an attempt to gain publicly what was never his privately. Nevertheless, in his interview with the *Sunday Tribune* and as also related by Brenda Power on RTE radio's *This Week* yesterday, he did make salient points.

It is likely that some suicides are not mentally ill. He believed that he was not. No one knows the proportion of suicides who are mentally ill, which in any case may not be constant in any society over time.

The given medical maxim in recent decades has been that all or virtually all are ill. This may not be so, however. A reading of history might lead one to think otherwise. Was Wolfe Tone ill when he cut his throat? I doubt it.

In 100 consecutive suicides assessed through attendance at the Coroners Courts in Cork city and subsequently by speaking to relatives and others, it was found, by us, that whereas 80 per cent of women had been medically treated in the months prior to their deaths, only half of the men had received such. With young males aged 15 to 24, the situation was even more striking. Only one in five had received treatment.[3]

What does this mean? It was possible that many were mentally ill but did not recognise it. Others may have been ill but did not seek treatment. Some may not have been ill at all. The reasons why and the proportions are presently being researched.

Pat Tierney, then, was right in his first point. Some of those who kill themselves are likely not to be mentally ill when they choose to do so. We do not know, however, whether Pat himself was psychologically ill at the time he ended his life. The fact that he arranged it meticulously does not prove that he was mentally well.

Many suicides who are mentally ill do just that. They outwit their relatives, friends, nurses and doctors, usually in contrast to Pat through secrecy rather than the public way he did it. In classical times publicised suicides were much more common.

Suicide and attempted suicide, since 1993, is no longer a criminal matter in Ireland. One consequence of this may be that the law, and in particular the police, is limited in how it might intervene. This was not always so.

In the last century attempted suicides in London were often confined to prison as a preventive measure. This was largely on advice given by prison chaplains to magistrates. They believed that they could prevent occurrence by moral persuasion.[4] They were not particularly successful and the practice gradually lapsed.

Recurrence remains a great problem, however, in spite of better-trained doctors, psychologists, voluntary workers and effective anti-depressants. For this reason the Suicide Research Foundation is endeavouring to develop new methods of treatment, where appropriate, and intervention.

Pat may have been wrong here, however. Most cases of attempted suicide do not go on to complete suicide. About 1 per cent do so in the subsequent year and between 10 to 15 per cent do so in the subsequent 10 to 15 years.

The importance of this is that Pat may have, unintentionally, provided a model for the suicidally ambivalent. Many would-be suicides are just that. Will I, won't I? Let chance or fate decide. Many young impressionable suicides are copy-cat.[5] The figure is estimated to be one in five in the United States.

Most if not all human acts have a moral component – how we buy, how we sell, how we drive, how we drink and how we communicate.[6] How we die must be added to this list.

What Pat did was legal. If it calls others forth to die then morally this would be an undesirable consequence. Yeats was very conscious of this effect of his 'sacrificial' writings, in later life.[7] We can induce death by example.

This raises the issue of publicising individual suicides, including the methods used and the attendant circumstances. The consensus among suicidologists is that there is a relationship between the 'dose' of publicity and the likelihood of imitation.

To be well-known, to be seen as an icon, to be on the front page, to be given banner headlines, to be discussed on major news and television programmes may be an inducement to the vulnerable.

To be criticised publicly for the act, yet not rejected as a loved individual, which was the approach of Courtney Love to the suicide of her husband Kurt Cobain, may be protective.

The news media, however, must be ever conscious of their power for good and for evil.[8] Last June another Sunday newspaper attributed, by implication, two suicides to the Leaving and Junior cert examinations which were concurrently in progress. This was wrong-headed. They associated a common experience, examinations, with an uncommon event, suicide. It was also, in my opinion, immoral.

Sufferers from AIDS may experience many psychological symptoms.[9] Dementia is one outcome as the illness advances, and depression is another which may occur at any time from learning of the positive blood test to the physical advancement of the illness. Pat was clearly not demented.

Whether he was depressed or not is another matter. In depression there are two sets of symptoms, objective, which include sleep disturbance, loss of appetite, a fall in weight, diminution of energy, daily variation in mood, and subjective.

The latter may be summarised as the future is hopeless, the world meaningless and the self worthless. He certainly saw the future as hopeless and for him the world had become meaningless. I do not know if he saw himself as less worthy or of less importance than when he had his full physical virility. The fact that he discussed his plans with Brenda Power does not mean he was not suffering from a depressive illness.

Many making serious suicide attempts will relate, afterwards, that once they had made up their minds the cloud lifted and they felt buoyant and almost elated in the knowledge they had decided to end their lives.

The importance of these possibilities relate to our moral responsibility once we know a friend or relative is suicidal. Do we have a responsibility to intervene to prevent the occurrence? A person can be compulsorily admitted to a mental hospital if mentally ill and suicidal. The law, however, relates to the mental illness and not the suicidal behaviour.

Relatives of one patient in Ireland wished the person retained compulsorily in a mental hospital because they believed she was suicidal. The patient wished to leave. The doctors after careful examination and prolonged observation could find no evidence of illness. They felt obliged under the Mental Treatment Act to discharge her. She later ended her life.

It would have been better in my opinion if Pat Tierney had seen someone professionally before he died. He might still have proceeded to kill himself. Yet we would know that some skilled professional person had assessed whether he was depressed or psychologically ill in any other way.

My mind goes back almost thirty years to a young highly intelligent Chinese philosophy student whom I treated in an emergency clinic at a psychiatric hospital in London.

She had made a serious attempt on her life and advanced many philosophical and social reasons why she should complete the event. I believed she was depressed and in danger of killing herself. She pleaded against compulsory admission, preferring to return to her lonely bedsit.

Agreement was reached. I reasoned that confinement would not protect her life in the long term. She would give treatment a chance – antidepressants and counselling – before acting against herself. She recovered. Subsequently she told me that philosophically she still thought life was not worth living. However, since her depression had lifted, she no longer felt like ending her life.

Finally, many in our society are physically sick with potentially fatal illnesses, whether cancer, AIDS, heart or lung disease.[9] Up to a third of these may be depressed.

Because of this they see the future as hopeless. Once they are successfully treated, however, the darkness dissipates. Pat Tierney may have wished his private self to die because of untreated depression or depression that did not respond to treatment.

He wished his public self, however, even in the absence of heaven, to continue, at least for a time in the minds of his friends and those, like me, who were made aware of his tragedy.

Michael Sheridan, who was previously a journalist with the *Irish Press*, wrote an illuminating article in the *Sunday Independent* on 14 January 1996. Pat Tierney had attempted the same previously, but this newspaper's response was different, which probably saved Pat's life at the time. He was set upon ending his life, but he wished a guarantee of publicity. Michael Sheridan refused to provide such a platform. Instead, he did very practical things, such as providing him with access to professional help.

He also confirmed my clinical suspicions, as outlined in the *Irish Times* article, that Pat Tierney was buoyant in an abnormal way when he outlined his suicide plan. The words used were 'manic elation'. Clearly, for Pat, the whole episode had the quality of high theatre. This is not

dissimilar to *iactatio*, the word given to describe some
contrived public suicides in classical times.

EPILOGUE

All God's creatures got a place in the choir
Some sing low and some sing higher
Some sing out loud on the telephone wire
And some just clap their hands, or paws or anything
    they've got now.

This well-known ballad strikes me as being a reinterpretation of the Sermon on the Mount, relevant to a modern Irish context. It reflects, unfortunately, an idealised aspiration rather than the crude reality. Many of the Irish do not have a place in the choir. In fact, from birth, many may have been written out altogether – no lines to say and no part to play.

The great challenge of education is to instil a sense of purpose, direction and commitment in an individual. As the very word implies, education should educe wisdom from an individual, rather than impose it on him. It goes beyond formal schooling and begins even earlier than the first playschool years

The relationship between the child and his mother, as expressed through eye contact and bodily contact, is extremely important. We first see ourselves reflected in the faces of others. We internalise the expressions of others in response to ourselves, and from this we develop our sense of worth and well-being. Grimacing and growling parents are likely to be incorporated into the internal worlds of their disgruntled children.

There is some evidence that the male brain is different to that of the female, maybe in infancy and perhaps even in the womb. Be this as it may, boys and girls are often treated differently from an early age. Clothes are carefully chosen according to the sex of a child, even from infancy. Indeed, boys and girls are still often dressed in blue and pink respectively. Toys are also chosen to reflect the expected or desired emotional differences between the sexes – hard, instrumental toys for boys with soft and cuddly ones for girls. The net result in boys may be an inhibition of emotion, apart from expression of ritualised aggression; while in girls the expression of broader emotional feelings may be encouraged and enhanced.

This stereotyping of gender role development, which is socially and culturally determined (albeit on the basis of genuine biological differences), may have the effect of facilitating or inhibiting emotional recognition. Boys may be less in touch with their own inner feelings than girls, apart from feelings of aggression and love.[1] They may be afraid to express feelings of depression or anxiety, which they see as shameful and falling short of the masculine ideal. For some, rather than living with uncertainty and the anticipation of weakness and failure in the future, it is easier to end it all now.

Disadvantage is unequally distributed in Ireland. This was very obvious in the rural Ireland of the last century and the early part of this century. Urban life now shows striking geographical differences. Redistribution of financial wealth through taxation is only part of the solution, if it is a solution at all.

Somehow the early life of our children, particularly deprived children, must be improved. However, this problem is likely to worsen rather than improve with changes in family life. One in five children now live in one-parent households.[2] This figure is higher in some urban areas of other countries. Unmarried mothers are likely to be younger and less educated than married mothers are. They are also more likely to be caught in a poverty trap. Such backgrounds may relate to high rates of parasuicide.[3]

Whereas illness was ignored by Durkheim and its importance denied in relation to suicide; it is quite possible that work done twenty or thirty years ago overstated the connection. Certainly, men (particularly young men) do not tend to come forward for treatment in the months before their deaths. Some of these may not have recognised their illness – the first episode of depression is often misunderstood and despondency is explained away by criticism of the world and one's own ability to deal with it. Patients need to be taught to recognise that they are ill, and not lazy or incompetent. Others may recognise this fact, but may be too proud or too sceptical to accept treatment. Still others may lack impulse-control and end their lives in response to a rebuff or perceived stress. The fact remains that the common link in all these cases is premature death.

Is it morbid to read a book such as this, or even more so, to write one? One American researcher, known to me, sought to study the possibility that suicidologists had a higher rate of suicide than those of similar backgrounds. The study proved impossible and inconclusive. Although suicides are rare, suicidologists are even rarer.

Life and death, however, are two reflections of the

same thing. Appreciation of individual existence presupposes a discontinuity with other individuals and also a discontinuity in time. If one accepts that there was a time when one did not exist, then clearly there will be a time when non-existence will supervene. No one understands what ultimately motivates the individual to shorten his life. Camus tells us that this is the ultimate philosophical question.[4]

For this reason, it seems strange to me that no philosopher of calibre has addressed the problem of suicide in the twentieth century. Wittgenstein is said to be the greatest philosopher of our time.[5] For much of his life he was very unhappy and often depressed. Three of his brothers committed suicide, as did one of his cousins: one brother drowned himself, one poisoned himself and one shot himself. Wittgenstein himself was rescued from a suicide attempt at a railway station, by his uncle, following the tragic accidental death of a very close friend.

During the First and Second World Wars, he insisted on working in situations where death was close at hand. He was Jewish, which for many years he and his family denied and, being Austrian, he fought on the losing side during the First World War. Like St Francis, but to an even greater extent, he was very wealthy until he gave it all away. This was a type of 'death to the world' which characterised religious vocation of an earlier era.

In spite of much hardship and many broken relationships, to which he more than contributed himself; Wittgenstein survived to write his great philosophical works before dying, aged 62, of cancer. If there were certainty in our knowledge – the combination of his personality, his illness, his parasuicidal behaviour, his brothers' deaths and the death of a childhood hero through suicide – should have all combined to induce a similar fate in Wittgenstein. Yet, it never happened. He himself believed that his discovery of Bertrand Russell's philosophy saved his life. Although he went on to quarrel with Russell, having first intimidated him; it is likely that this love of knowledge, which is what philosophy means, saved his life and ennobled ours.

This book commenced with the consideration of one great person, Terence MacSwiney, and ended with that of another, Ludwig Wittgenstein. The former had many reasons for living and yet, starved himself to death; whilst the latter had many reasons to kill himself and yet, lived. Such is the enigma of suicide.

REFERENCES

INTRODUCTION

1. Rosen, G., 'History in the study of suicide', *Psychological Medicine*, 1971; 1: pp. 267–285.
2. Battin, M.P., *Ethical issues in suicide*, New Jersey: Prentice Hall, 1995 (p. 168).
3. *Ibid.*, p. 169.
4. van Hooff, A.J., *From Autothanasia to Suicide: Self-killing in Classical Antiquity*, London: Routledge, 1990 (p. 174).
5. *Ibid*, p. 128.
6. *Ibid.*, p. 41.
7. Costello, F.J., *Enduring the most: the life and death of Terence MacSwiney*, Dingle: Brandon Press, 1995.
8. Briggs, A., *The Age of Improvement 1783–1867*, London: Longman, 1990 (p. 184).
9. Ellmann, M., *The Hunger Artists*, London: Virgo Press, 1993.
10 *Ibid.*, p. 17.

CHAPTER 1

1. Kirwan, P., 'Suicide in a Rural Irish Population', *Irish Medical Journal*, 1991; 84: pp. 14–15.
2. McCarthy, P.D. & Walsh, D., 'Suicide in Dublin', *British Medical Journal*, 1966; 1: pp. 1393–6.
3. Clarke-Finnegan, M. & Fahy, T.J., 'Suicide Rates in Ireland', *Psychological Medicine*, 1983; 13: pp. 385–391.
4. O'Donnell, I. & Farmer, R., 'The limitations of official suicide statistics', *British Journal of Psychiatry*, 1995; 166: pp. 458–461.
5. Garvey, D., *Suicide Statistics, Southern Health Board, 1987–1988*, Dublin: Central Statistics Office.
6. Kelleher, M.J., 'Suicide in Ireland', *Irish Medical Journal* 1991; 84 (2).
7. Kelleher, M.J., Corcoran, P., Keeley, H.S., Dennehy, J., & O'Donnell, I., 'Improving procedures for recording suicide statistics', *Irish Medical Journal*, 1996.

8. Sainsbury, P., & Barraclough, B., 'Differences between suicide rates', *Nature*, 1968; 220: p. 1252.

9. Lester, D., 'Migration and Suicide', *Medical Journal of Australia*, 1972; 1: pp. 94–2.

10. Daly, M. & Kelleher, M.J., 'The increase in the suicide rate in Ireland', *Irish Medical Journal*, 1987; 80 (8): pp. 233–234.

11. Kelleher, M.J., Daly, M. & Kelleher, M.J.A., 'The influence of antidepressants in overdose on the increased suicide rate in Ireland between 1971 and 1988', *British Journal of Psychiatry*, 1992; 161: pp. 625–628.

12. Walsh, D., Cullen, A., Cullivan, R. & O'Donnell, B., 'Do statistics lie? Suicide in Kildare and in Ireland', *Psychological Medicine*, 1990; 20: pp. 867–871.

13. Kelleher, M.J., Corcoran, P. & Keohane, B., 'Suicide, cancer and road traffic accidents among the young in Ireland', *Irish Medical Journal*, 1995; 88: pp. 96–98.

14. Moksony, F., 'Place of birth and suicide in Hungary: a case control study', Paper presented at the Eighteenth Congress of the International Association for Suicide Prevention; Venice, Italy, 1995

15. Hess, L.E., 'Changing family patterns in Western Europe', in Rutter, M. & Smith, D.J. (Eds), *Psychosocial disorders in young people*, Chichester: Wiley (pp. 156–158).

16. Klerman, G.L. & Wiseman, M.M., 'Increasing rates of depression', *Journal of American Medical Association*, 1989; 261: pp. 2229–2235.

17. Fombonne, E., 'Depressive disorders: time trends and possible explanatory mechanisms', in Rutter, M. & Smith, D.J. (Eds), *Psychosocial disorders in young people*, Chichester: Wiley, pp. 579–580.

18. Kelleher, M.J., Keohane, B., Corcoran, P., Keeley, H., *Elderly Suicides in Ireland*, in press.

19. Kelleher, M.J., Keohane, B., Corcoran, P., Keeley, H., *One Hundred Irish Suicides: a psychological Autopsy Study*, in press.

CHAPTER 2

1. Durkheim, E., *Suicide: a study in sociology*. Translated by Spaulding, J.A. & Simpson, G. Routledge. First published

1952. Present quotations from 1993 edition, p. 154.

2. *Ibid.*, p. 152–156.

3. Kerkhof, A. & Kunst, A., 'A European perspective on suicidal behaviour', in Jenkins, R., *et al* (Eds), *The prevention of suicide*, London: HMSO, (pp. 22–23).

4. Sainsbury, P. & Barraclough, B., 'Differences between suicide rates', *Nature*, 1968; pp. 220–1252.

5. Diekstra, R.F.W., 'On the burden of suicide', in Kelleher M.J., (Ed.), *Divergent perspectives on suicidal behaviour*, Proceedings of Fifth European Symposium on Suicide, Cork 1994.

6. Mac Gréil, M., *Religious practice and attitudes in Ireland*, Published by the Survey and Research Unit, Department of Social Studies, St Patrick's College, Maynooth, Co. Kildare 1991.

7. Retterstøl, N., *Suicide, a European perspective*, New York: Cambridge University Press, 1993 (pp. 25–27).

8. Breslin, A. & Weafer, J.A., *Religious beliefs, practice and moral attitudes: a comparison of two surveys, 1974–1984*, Maynooth: Council for Research and Development.

9. *Sunday Independent/Late Late Show* IMS Poll. *Sunday Independent*, 1995; 9 (45): p. 9.

10. Retterstøl, N., *Suicide: a European perspective*, New York: Cambridge University Press, 1993 (p. 17).

11. Ialaluddin, Umri, 'Suicide or termination of life', Translated from the Urdu by SAH Rizvi, *Islamic and Comparative Law*. Quarterly 1987; 7: pp. 136–145.

12. Cavan, R., *Suicide* (pp. 65–66), New York: Russell & Russell, 1965.

13. Frend, W.C., *The Donatist Church*, Oxford: Clarendon, 1952 (p. 175).

14. Greenstone, J.H., 'Martyrdom', in *Encyclopaedia Judiaca*; 15: pp. 490–1. Jerusalem: Keter, 1971.

CHAPTER 3

1. Freud, S., *Totem and Taboo*, Translated by Strackey, J. London: Routledge, 1950.

2. Durkheim, E., *The elementary forms of the religious life: a study in religious sociology*, Translated by Swain, J.W. London & New York: Macmillan, 1915 (pp. 236–7).

3. Thompson, K., *Key Sociologists: Emile Durkheim*, Series Editor: Peter Hamilton, The Open University, Milton Keynes. London: Routledge (pp. 109–116).

4. Corkery, D., *The Hidden Ireland*, Dublin: Gill & Macmillian, 1924.

5. Vital statistics quarterly report: yearly summary, 1971–1992, Central Statistics Office.

6. Report of An Bord Uchtala, 1993, Department of Health. Government Publication.

7. Barraclough, B., 'The suicidal patient: scope for preventive action', *Modern Medicine of Ireland*, 1988; pp. 15–19.

8. Kelleher, M.J., 'Cross-national (Anglo-Irish) differences in obsessional symptoms and traits of personality', *Psychological Medicine*, 1972; 2(1): pp. 33–41.

9. Durkheim, E., *Suicide: a study in sociology*, Translated by Spalding, J.A. & Simpson, G. London: Routledge, 1993 (pp. 188–189).

10. Hess, L.E., 'Changing family patterns in Western Europe', in Rutter, M. & Smith, D.J., *Psychosocial disorders in young people*, Chichester: John Wiley, 1995.

11. Rotheram-Borus, M.J. & Fernardez, M.I., 'Sexual orientation and developmental challenges experienced by gay and lesbian youths', *Suicide and Life-Threatening Behaviour* (suppl.) 1995; 25: pp. 26–34.

12. Muechrer, P., 'Suicide and sexual orientation: a critical summary of recent research and directions for future research', *Suicide and Life-Threatening Behaviour* (suppl.) 1995; 25: pp. 72–81.

13. Robinson, W.S., 'Ecological correlations and the behaviour of individuals', *American Sociological Review*, 1950; 15: pp. 351–357.

14. Hamishek, E.A., Jackson, J.E. & Kan, J.F., 'Model specification: use of aggregate data and the ecological correlation fallacy', *Political Methodology*, 1974; Winter: pp. 89–107.

CHAPTER 4

1. Kelleher, M.J., Corcoran, P. & Keohane, B., 'Suicide, cancer and road traffic accidents among the young in Ireland', *Irish Medical Journal*, 1995; 88: pp. 96–98.

2. Department of Education: statistical report, 1976–1990. Government Publication.

3. Durkheim, E., *A study in sociology*, Translated by Spalding, J.A. & Simpson, G., London: Routledge, 1993 (pp. 164–168).

4. Kerkhof, A. & Kunst, A., 'A European perspective on suicidal behaviour', in *The prevention of suicide*, edited by Jenkins, R., *et al*, London: HMSO.

5. Goleman, D., *Emotional intelligence* – to be published by Bloomsbury, 1996. Reported in *News Review of Sunday Times*, 22 October 1995.

6. Barraclough, B., Bunch, J., Nelson, B. & Sainsbury, P., 'A hundred cases of suicide: clinical aspects', *British Journal of Psychiatry*, 1974; 125: pp. 355–373.

7. O'Dwyer, A.M,. Sheppard, M.P., Murphy, M.N. & Horgan, R., 'A catchment area study of suicides in Waterford in 1990', *Irish Journal of Psychological Medicine*, 1992; 9: pp. 108–110.

8. Balldin, Z., Berggren, U., Engel, J. & Eriksson, M., 'Neurodoctrine evidence for reduced serotinergic neurotransmission during heavy drinking', *Alcoholism, clinical and experimental research*, 1994; 18 (4): pp. 822–825.

9. Traskman-Bendz, L, Eriksson J., Nimeus, A. & Regnell, G., 'Understanding suicidal behaviour from a biological viewpoint', in *Divergent perspectives on suicidal behaviour*, Proceedings of the Fifth European Symposium on Suicide, 1994, Cork.

Chapter 5

1. Paerregaard, G., *Selvmord og selvmordsforsog i Kobenhavn* (Suicide and Attempted Suicide), Bin 1, 2 og 3, Copenhagen: Munksgaard, 1963.

2. Beskow, J., 'Suicide and mental disorder in Swedish men', *Acta Psychiatrica Scandinavica* (Suppl.), 1979; p. 27.

3. Retterstøl, N., Ekeland, H. & Hesso, R., *Suicide among the young: development in Norway. A seven year study from Oslo*, Tidssknor Laegeforen 1989; 105: pp. 119–122.

4. Retterstøl, N., *Suicide: a European perspective*, New York: Cambridge University Press, 1993 (pp. 106–113).

5. Barraclough, B., Bunch, J., Nelson, B., & Sainsbury, P., 'A hundred cases of suicide: clinical aspects', *British Journal of Psychiatry*, 1974; 125: pp. 355–373.

6. Kelleher, M.J., Keohane, B. & Corcoran, P., *One hundred Cork Suicides*, in press.

7. Dr Marie O' Sullivan: personal communication.

8. Shaffer, D., Gould, M., Hicks, R., 'Epidemiology, mechanisms and clinical features of youth suicide', in Kelleher, M.J. (Ed.), *Divergent Perspectives on Suicidal Behaviour*, Proceedings of Fifth European Symposium on Suicide, 1994 (pp. 79–95).

9. Charlton, J., Kelly, S., Dunnell, K., Evans, B,. Jenkins, R. & Wallis, R., 'Trends in suicide deaths in England and Wales: trends in factors associated with suicide death.', in Jenkins, R., *et al* (Eds), *The Prevention of Suicide*, London: HMSO, 1994 (pp. 5–22).

10. Hawton, K., 'Assessment of suicide risk', *British Journal of Psychiatry*, 1987; 150: pp. 145–153.

11. Priest, R.G., 'Improving the management and knowledge of depression', *British Journal of Psychiatry*, 1994; 164: pp. 284–287.

12. Rutz, W., von Knorring, L. & Walinder, J., 'Long-term effects of an educational programme for general practitioners given by the Swedish Committee for the Prevention and Treatment of Depression', *Acta Psychiatrica Scandinavica*, 1992; 85: pp. 83–88.

CHAPTER 6

1. Kreitman, N., 'Suicide and parasuicide', in Kendell, R.E. & Zealley, A.K., *Companion to psychiatric studies*, Churchill Livingstone, 1993.

2. World Health Organisation, *Working group on preventative practices in suicide and attempted suicide, summary report* (ICP/PSF 017 652V), Copenhagen WHO Regional Office for Europe.

3. Daly, M., Conway, M. & Kelleher, M.J., 'Social determinants of self-poisoning', *British Journal of Psychiatry*, 1986; 148: pp. 406–413.

4. Kelleher, M.J., Kelleher, M.J.A., Corcoran, P., Daly, M., Daly, F. & Crowley, M.J., *Parasuicide, poverty and public health*, in press.

5. Benzeval, M., Judge, K. & Whitehead, M., *Tackling inequalities in health: an agenda for action*, London: Kings Fund, 1995.

6. Tremblay, R.E., Pihl, R.O., Vitaro, F. & Dobkin, P.L., 'Predicting early onset of male antisocial behaviour from preschool behaviour', *Archives of General Psychiatry*, 1994; 51: pp. 732–739.

Chapter 7

1. Kelleher, M.J., Daly, M., Keohane, B., Daly, C., Daly, F., Crowley, M.J. & Kelleher, M.J.A., 'Deprivation and long term outcome of deliberate self-poisoning', in Kelleher, M.J. (Ed.), *Divergent Perspectives on Suicidal Behaviour*, Proceedings of Fifth European Symposium on Suicide, Cork, 1994 (pp. 71–78).

2. Ritson, E.B., Chick, J.D. & Strang, J., 'Dependence on alcohol and other drugs', in Kendell, K.E. & Zeally, A.K. (Eds), *Companion to Psychiatric Studies*, London: Churchill Livingstown (p. 374).

3. Kreitman, N. & Casey, P., 'The repitition of parasuicide: an epidemiological and clinical study', *British Journal of Psychiatry*, 1988; 153: pp. 792–800.

4. Rutter, M. & Madge, N., *Cycles of disadvantage: a review of research*, London: Heinemann, 1976.

5. Gunnell, D.J., Peters, T.J., Kammerling, R.M. & Brooks, J., 'Relation between parasuicide, suicide, psychiatric admissions and socio-economic deprivation', *British Medical Journal*, 1995; 311: pp. 226–230.

Chapter 8

1. Garvey, D., *Suicide statistics, Southern Health Board 1987/88*, Dublin: Central Statistics Office.

2. Vollman, R.R., Ganzert, A., *et al*, 'The reactions of family systems to sudden and unexpected death', *Omega*, 1971; 2: pp. 101–106.

3. Kelleher, M.J., 'Death by suicide', in Keane, C. (Ed.), *Death and Dying*, Dublin/Cork: Mercier Press, 1995.

Chapter 9

1. Daly, M., Conway, M., & Kelleher, M.J., 'Social determinants of self-poisoning', *British Journal of Psychiatry*, 1986; 148: pp. 406–413.

2. Kelleher, M.J., Kelleher, M.J.A., Corcoran, P., Daly, M., Daly, F., & Crowley, M.J., *Parasuicide, Poverty and Public Health*, in press.

3. Goldacre, M., Deagroatt, V. & Hawton, K., 'Suicide after discharge from psychiatric inpatient care', *The Lancet*, 1993; 342: pp. 283–286.

4. Bowers, F., *Suicide in Ireland*, Dublin; Irish Medical Organisation, 1994.

5. Anderson, O., *Suicide in Victorian and Edwardian England*, Oxford: Clarendon Press, 1987 (p. 322).

6. Bronish, T., 'Prospective longterm follow-up of suicide attempters', in Crepet, P., Ferrari, G., Platt, S. & Bellini, M. (Eds), *Suicidal behaviour in Europe*, Rome: John Lilly, 1992 (p. 179).

7. Lester, D., *Questions and answers about suicide*, Philadelphia: The Charles Press, 1989 (p. 81).

8. *Bunreacht na hÉireann (Constitution of Ireland)*, (pp. 126–138), Dublin: Government Publications Sales Office, 1937.

9. Kreitman, N., 'Suicide and parasuicide', in Kendall, R.E. & Zeally, A.K. (Eds), *Companion to Psychiatric Studies*, London: Churchill Livingstone, 1993 (p. 757).

10. Kelleher, M.J., Corcoran, P., & Keohane, B., 'Suicide, cancer and road traffic accidents among the young in Ireland, *Irish Medical Journal*, 1995; 88: pp. 96–98.

11. Durkheim, E., *The rules of sociological method*, Translation by Solovay, S.A. & Mueller J.; Chicago: University of Chicago Free Press, 1938 (p. 64).

12. Morton, M., Silverman, M.D., & Maris, R.W., 'The prevention of suicidal behaviours: an overview', *Suicide and Life Threatening Behaviour*, 1995; 25 (1): pp. 10–21.

13. Haddon, W., 'The changing approach to the epidemiology, prevention and amelioration of trauma: the transition to approaches etiologically rather than descriptively based', *American Journal of Public Health*, 1968; 58: pp. 1431–1438.

14. Haddon, W., Baker, S.P., 'Injury Control', in Clarke, D.W., MacMahon, B. (eds), *Prentative and community medicine*, Boston: Little, Brown, 1981, pp. 109–140.

15. Center for Disease Control (CDC), 'Recommendations for a

community plan for the prevention and containment of suicide clusters', *Morbidity and Mortality Weekly*, 1988; 37: pp. 1–12.

16. Phillips, D.P., 'The Werther Effect: suicide and other forms of violence are contagious', *The Sciences*, 1985; 25 (4): pp. 32–39.

17. Shaffer, D. & Bacon, K., 'A critical review of preventative intervention efforts in suicide, with particular reference to youth suicide', in *Prevention and interventions in youth suicide Report of the Secretary's Task Force on youth suicide*, Vol. 3, Publication No:89/1623, Washington D.C, 1989 (pp. 31–61).

18. Priest, R.G., 'Improving the management and knowledge of depression', *British Journal of Psychiatry*, 1994; 164: pp. 285–287.

19. McLeavey, B., Kelleher, M.J., Mitchell, C., Carey, M. & Devane, E., *Interpersonal problem-solving training by nurse therapists for parasuidical patients*, in press.

20. Morgan, H.G., *Death wishes? The understanding and management of deliberate self-harm*, New York: John Wiley, 1979.

21. Traskman-Bendz, L,. Eriksson, J., Nimeus, A. & Regnell, G., 'Understanding suicidal behaviour from a biological viewpoint', in Kelleher, M.J. (Ed.), *Divergent perspectives on suicidal behaviour*, Proceedings of the Fifth European Symposium on Suicide, Cork, 1994.

22. Keeley, H.S., Nolan, M., Kelleher, M.J. & Duane, M., *Is platelet Serotoinin aggregation a relevant marker for depressive states or traits? A pilot study of normal and depressed subjects*, paper presented at trainees day, Royal Society of Medicine, 1994.

23. Keeley, H.S., Nolan, M., Hooley, K,. Morgan, E. & Kelleher, M.J., 'Is there a peripheral marker of suicidality? A pilot study of auto-aggressive males', in *Divergent Perspectives on Suicidal Behaviour*, Proceedings of the Fifth European Symposium on Suicidal Behaviour, Cork, 1994.

24. Kelleher, M.J. & Shanahan, F., 'Psychoneuroimmunology and suicidal behaviour', *Irish Medical Journal*, 1995; 88 (1): pp. 18–23.

CHAPTER 10

1. Fitzpatrick, C., 'Diagnosis of depressive disorders in the adolescent', *Irish Medical Times* (Depression Supplement), 1995; pp. 8–9.

2. Shaffer, D., Garland, A., Gould, M., Fisher, P. & Trautman, P., 'Preventing teenage suicide: a critical review', *Journal of the American Academy of Child and Adolescent Psychiatry*, 1988; 27 (6): pp. 675–687.

3. Retterstøl, N., *Suicide: a Europe perspective*, New York: Cambridge University Press, 1993 (pp. 25–27).

4. Kelleher, M.J., Keohane, B. & Corcoran, P., *One Hundred Cork Suicides*, in press.

5. Leffert, N. & Petersen, A.C., 'Patterns of development during adolescence' in Rutter, M. & Smith, D.J. (Eds), *Psychosocial disorders in young people*, Chichester: John Wiley, 1995.

6. Diekstra, R.F.W., 'Epidemiology of suicide: aspects of definition, classification and prevention policies', in Crepet, P., Ferrari, G., Platt, S. & Bellini, M. (Eds), *Suicidal behaviour in Europe, recent research findings*, Rome: John Libby, 1992.

CHAPTER 11

1. Pijnenborg, L., van Delden, J.J.M., Kardaun, J.W.P.F., Glerum, J.J. & van der Maas, P.J., 'Nationwide study of decisions concerning the end of life in general practice in the Netherlands', *British Medical Journal*, 1994; 309: pp. 1209–1212.

2. Foster, R.F., *Modern Ireland*, London: Penguin, 1989 (pp. 279–280).

3. Briggs, A., *The Age of Improvement 1783–1867*, Longman, 1990 (p. 184).

4. Barraclough, B.M., 'The Bible suicides', *Acta Psychiatrica Scandinavica*, 1992; 86: pp. 64–69.

5. Retterstøl, N., *Suicide: a European perspective*, New York: Cambridge University Press, 1993 (p. 17).

6. Greenstone, J.H., 'Martyrdom', in *Encyclopaedia Judacea*, Vol.15, Jerusalem: Keter, 1971 (pp. 490–491).

7. Rosen, G., 'History in the study of suicide', *Psychological Medicine*, 1971; 1: pp. 267–285.

8. Battin, M.P., *Ethical issues in suicide*, New Jersey: Prentice Hall, 1995 (p. 64).

9. Dworkin, R., *Life's dominion: an argument about abortion*, *euthanasia and individual freedom*, New York: Knops, 1993.

10. van Hooff, A.J.L., *From autothanasia to suicide: self-killing in classical antiquity*, London: Routledge, 1990 (pp. 195–196).

11. Warnock, M., *The uses of philosopy*, Oxford: Blackwell, 1992 (pp. 41–45).

12. Graham, G., 'Suicide and voluntary euthanasia: a moral philosophical perspective', in Kelleher, M.J. (Ed.), *Divergent perspectives on suicidal behaviour*, Proceedings of the Fifth European Symposium on Suicide, Cork, 1994.

13. Kelleher, M.J., 'Euthanasia, assisted suicide and suicide', *Irish Medical Journal*, 1992; 85 (4): p. 125.

14. Kelleher, M.J., *Suicide: ethical considerations*, in press.

15. Kelleher, M.J., A critical review of the Dutch television film *Death on Request*, *Crisis* 1995; 16 (3): p.141.

CHAPTER 12

1. Tierney, P., *The Moon on My Back*, Dublin: Seven Towers, 1993

2. Power, B., *The Sunday Tribune*, 7 November 1995.

3. Kelleher, M.J., Keohane, B., Corcoran, P., *One Hundred Cork Suicides*, in press.

4. Anderson, O., *Suicide in Victorian and Edwardian England*, Oxford: Clarendon Press, 1987.

5. Kreitman, N., 'Suicide and parasuicide', in Kendell, R.E. & Zeally, A.K. (Eds), *Companion to Psychiatric Studies*, London: Churchill Livingstone, 1993.

6. Kelleher, M.J., *Suicide: ethical implications*, in press.

7. Yeats, W.B., 'The king's threshold' in *Collected Plays*, London: Macmillan, 1982.

8. Wartella, E., 'Media and problem behaviour in young people', in Rutter, M. & Smith, D.G. (Eds), *Psychosocial disorders in young people*, Chichester: John Wiley, 1995.

9. Catalan, J., Seyas, D., Lief, J., Pergami, A. & Burgess, A., 'Suicidal behaviour in HIV infection: a case-control study of deliberate self-harm in people with HIV infection', *Archives of Suicide Research*, 1995; 1(2): pp. 85–96.

10. van Hooff, A.J., *From Autothanasia to Suicide: Self-killing in Classical Antiquity*, London: Routledge, 1990 (p. 37).

EPILOGUE

1. Goleman, D., Emotional intelligence, To be published by Bloomsbury, reported in News Review of *Sunday Times*, 22 October 1995.

2. Courtney, D., 'The changing demography of Irish women in the 1980s', Proceedings of the Strasbourg Council of Europe Seminar, *Present Demographic Trends and Lifestyles in Europe*, 1991; pp. 347–349.

3. Kelleher, M.J., Kelleher, M.J.A., Corcoran, P., Daly, M., Daly, F. & Crowley, M.J., *Parasuicide, poverty and public health*, in press.

4. Camus, A., 'The myth of Sisyphus', in Miller, (Ed.), *On suicide*, San Francisco: Chronicle Books, 1992 (pp. 107–116).

5. Monk, R, Ludwig, Wittgenstein, *The duty of genius*, London: Vintage, 1991.

TABLE OF FIGURES/TABLES

All but two (tables 2.1 and 2.2) of the illustrations shown in this book have been produced by the Suicide Research Foundation. In each case, the source(s) of the data is stated clearly. Tables 2.1 and 2.2 have been adapted from the Breslin & Weafer and Mac Gréil books.

SUBJECT AND TERM INDEX

83–4, 86–94, 113
family life, 34, 115
media, 83, 108
mental health, 48–9, 84,
105–6, 114–5
prayer habits, 28

puberty, 21, 50
sexuality, 35
stress, 37, 81
suicide rates, 37–40, 42–
4, 49, 88
unemployment, 42–3

NAME INDEX

Recovery Incorporated (Ireland), 91, 93
Russell, Bertrand, 117

Samaritans (the), 78, 81, 90, 94
Samson, 10
Sands, Bobby, 13
Saul, 10
Schizophrenia Association, 91, 94
Seneca, 98
Sheridan, Michael, 111
Southern Health Board, 16, 69
St Augustine, 26, 29, 97, 99–100
St Brendan's Hospital, 103
St Francis, 116
St Thomas Aquinas, 99

St Vincent's Hospital, 103

Suicide Research Foundation, 22, 47, 84–5, 87, 107
Sunday Independent, 29, 111
Sunday Tribune, 103–5

Tertullian, 98
Tierney, Pat, 103–12

Weafer, J. A., 26–7
Wittgenstein, Ludwig, 116–7
Wolfe Tone, 96, 105
World Health Organisation (WHO), 53

Yeats, William, Butler, 107–8

Zimri, 10

More Interesting Books

NERVOUS BREAKDOWN
EDITED BY COLM KEANE

Most Irish families have at one time or another been affected by the bewildering consequences of 'nervous breakdown'. The symptoms and manifestations inculde depression, panic attacks, addictions, phobias, obsessions, sexual problems and difficulties eating and sleeping. These may result from anxiety, stress, trauma, family pressures, or from events such as job loss or bereavement. If you or your family have experienced any of these problems then this book will be of interest to you.

Nervous Breakdown is a companion to the RTE Radio 1 series of the same name. The book is prepared in an 'easy to read' style and is aimed at the non-expert. It offers simple advice on how to cope with the pressures and stresses of everyday life and it gives practical advice on the treatments.

Contributors include some of Ireland's most eminent psychologists, psychiatrists and therapists.

DEATH AND DYING

EDITED BY COLM KEANE

Death and Dying examines the Irish response to bereavement, grief and mourning. Drawing on Irish experts, the book explores normal and abnormal reactions to the death of a spouse, parent child or loved one. The sensitive issues of suicide, violent death and death by choice are also examined.

Death and Dying is a companion to the RTE Radio 1 series of the same name. The book offers simple guidance on how to cope with bereavement as well as practical advice on where to go for help.

The contributors – some of Ireland's most eminent bereavement experts – include psychologists, psychiatrists and medical specialists.

THE LOVE CRUCIBLE

SUSAN LINDSAY

Our world is hungry for love. The author of *The Love Crucible* believes that it is possible for individuals to recover and develop the power to love in their own lives. The crucible of the title represents the process by which the individual is transformed and enabled to find a deeper love. Such potential exists in all stages of human life. The topics covered in detail in *The Love Crucible* include:

- *Recovering the ability to love*
- *Love as a development process*
- *Good communication: the dialogue of love*
- *Imagery: a language for the soul*
- *Mediation: coming home to love.*

MORTALLY WOUNDED
STORIES OF SOUL PAIN, DEATH AND HEALING

MICHAEL KEARNEY

Mortally Wounded explores the nature of soul pain and the healing in those close to death. Drawing on his extensive experience of caring for people who are terminally ill, Michael Kearney shares and reflects on the stories of a number of individuals. He develops a theory and technique of inner care based on mythological and psychological models, believing that such care is the essential complement to the physical or outer care of the patient. It can, he believes, 'enable the person to find his or her own way through the prison of soul pain to a place of greater wholeness, a new depth of living and a falling away of fear'.